THE
BUSINESS
OF
CREATIVITY

Dream, Believe, and Create the Life and Career You Want

PHILIY PAGE

BALBOA.
PRESS
A DIVISION OF HAY HOUSE

Balboa Press books may be ordered through booksellers or by contacting:

Balboa Press
A Division of Hay House
1663 Liberty Drive
Bloomington, IN 47403
www.balboapress.co.uk
1 (877) 407-4847

Print information available on the last page.

ISBN: 978-1-9822-8054-3 (sc)
ISBN: 978-1-9822-8056-7 (hc)
ISBN: 978-1-9822-8055-0 (e)

Balboa Press rev. date: 03/12/2019

Contents

For Paul and Huxley my dream team.

Introduction

I am so happy that you have chosen to pick up this book. I wrote this book to help women like you, and to dispel the myth of the starving artist. If you have ever wanted to have a career in the creative industries, or set up your own creative business, this book was written for you.

I have worked in the creative industries for over 24 years as an award-winning photojournalist, in advertising, documentaries, book publishing, picture editing, and feature films to name a few! I now run Creative Women International ® supporting women like you to build sustainable creative careers.

When I started the world looked very different from the world we live in today. There were no smartphones, no Facebook or Instagram. Portfolio careers were something alien, but I knew that I didn't want a 9-5 job in an office. The idea of remote working was something only journalists on assignment did. Today I work remotely from my laptop and train creatives in countries like the Ukraine, Brazil, and Turkey from my studio via Skype.

I have had the pleasure of watching creatives like you build amazing careers, and choose the type of life they want to live. I curated my career in the way that I wanted it to be, *and I know that you can too.*

When you start to read this book, I want you to have a notebook to hand. Put your digital gadgets away and return to paper. The act of opening a page and slowing down, allows your brain to process at a different rate. I believe that it opens up the 'dreaming area' of the brain. This book is about dreaming, believing, and making the life and career that you want. I also want you to look after your mental health, find support, and I'm here to help you make a career that you are proud of, and in for the long run.

I'm excited to take this journey with you and grateful that you have chosen me as your guide.

You can find more support at www.CreativeWomenInternational.com

1

Confidence

When I started on my career path as a young woman, I was terribly shy. I would look at the ground when walking down the street and constantly undersold myself and the talent I possessed. There wasn't a huge light bulb moment when I suddenly became confident overnight. It was more a series of trials and errors until I found myself standing in front of a room full of people to deliver a talk and realised that I wasn't scared.

Now don't get me wrong- I do have many days when I wake up and do not feel confident. But I have worked out tricks and ways of making myself more confident, and I want to share them with you.

Let us start with why we don't feel confident and work towards how we can fix that. Being unconfident, shy, or fearful shouldn't stop you from creating a career that you love or earning money from your talents. It's all a matter of how you deal with it and what your goals are. We'll talk more about that later.

When we don't feel confident, we have a flurry of emotions. We might feel fear or, embarrassment that we shouldn't be there, that we don't know enough, or that we will make fools of ourselves. These are perfectly natural emotions, and it is what we do with them that matters.

Women often feel under qualified for certain situations. Having gone to all-female schools, I know the pressure that is placed on women to study hard and get good grades. We are taught to remember facts and behave. I was one of the 'good girls' at school, but I admired those who rocked the boat. Their energy and enthusiasm for making changes to the rigid rules and educational system inspired me. Why were we being told to sit still, learn the facts, and not cause trouble? Obviously, we don't want a school full of over-opinionated, hormonal teenagers, but those high-spirited girls were on to something.

During my career, I have worked as a secondary school teacher in inner-city London and as a university lecturer, teaching boys and girls, and men and women. What I see time and time again are the girls studying hard, making notes, and making sure that they have all the bits of paper and information they need to get good grades. The boys, on the other hand, will ask for extra details, question if there is an opportunity they could be put forward for, and have an opinion in class. But they will privately ask me questions afterwards to fill in their knowledge gaps. Now, I am, of course, making a sweeping generalisation, as there are always exceptions to the rule.

What I have noticed, though, – is that if an opportunity is presented for male and female students to take part in, the male students will say yes and then worry about whether they are qualified enough. Whereas the female students will turn the opportunity down, saying that they aren't qualified enough or, don't have enough experience. Or else, they are too scared to try.

Having grown up in an all-male household, raised by my father and four brothers, I have seen this gung-ho attitude in men throughout my life. My brothers will set themselves up for jobs that push the boundaries of their knowledge and experience. They will learn on the job, or say yes to opportunities and figure it out afterwards. It can be pretty inspiring to watch.

As women, what would happen if we started saying yes to things before we were ready?

What if we got a grip on our fears and put ourselves forward more often, as an expert, talent, or trainer?

How does that make you feel? Scared, excited, or as if you want to dive back under the duvet?

As women, we are taught from a young age to behave, do our work, and not cause trouble: our educational experience rewards perfection and well-presented course-work. We become experts at research, but not necessarily good at presenting new ideas or speaking up for the knowledge we already have.

I want you to think back to a time at school, college, or university when you received praise for the work you did. If you can't remember a moment from your educational life, choose something from your personal life. Think back to that moment and how the praise made you feel. Did you feel proud of the work you did? Did you value the person giving the feedback? Did you believe the individual or did you pick holes in the praise given to you?

Confidence starts when we acknowledge the praise we receive even if it is a compliment about your hair, gift giving, or the way you organised an event.

When we say, "Oh, it was nothing," or, "Oh, this old thing?", we are telling the person giving us the gift of a compliment that we don't want it. How would you feel if someone had taken a beautiful birthday gift that you had chosen for him or her and then handed it back to you without unwrapping it and said, "I don't want it,"? I'm pretty sure you would feel awful and uncomfortable, standing there with the gift in your hands, and not knowing what to do with it. That is the same feeling you get when you hand someone a compliment, and the person bats it back to you in a negative way.

Learning to receive positively and thankfully, and listening to

3

the praise you receive, can help you on your journey to becoming more confident.

I'm going to set you a challenge this week to start your confidence building. You might believe that you are a confident person, but give it a go. You will still learn something from it, and it might help you to see things from another's point of view, or help you to coach someone who isn't confident.

I'm all about helping someone else along the way. We need to build up our sisterhood.

Challenge 1

This week give someone you know a compliment. It can be about the person's appearance, something she or he did, or something this individual helped you with. Take note of how the person responds to your praise, and how their response makes you feel.

The second part of the challenge is to compliment a stranger and take note of that person's, and your feelings when he or she responds to you. Write down those responses.

Confidence has many guises. It is not only how you feel inside, but also how you respond to others. Take note in your day how you interact with others. Is it positively or negatively? Could you make small adjustments to turn your interactions into a more positive experience? We all have terrible days. We shout at the driver who cuts us up at the junction, or we are grumpy with our partners when things haven't gone well at work. This is natural. I'm not talking about turning ourselves into smiling robots; I'm asking us to take a moment to check our responses to things.

Maybe that driver had an emergency to get to. Or the person was a jerk, and actually, it's better to have that driver in front of us, rather than tailgating our bumper. That rubbish day at work has got us down. Could we take a quick walk before we head home to clear our thoughts before we dump on our partners or flatmates? Or could we explain that we have had a bad day and ask for some advice or a hug? There's nothing wrong with feeling vulnerable and asking for a hug. If hugs aren't your thing, a friendly ear to chat events over can work wonders as well. We are only human. We spend our whole lives adjusting to our environments, experiences, and emotions.

As Henry Miller said-
"Even if our whole life was a mistake, there is always time to change."

You might wonder what on earth compliment taking, and being vulnerable has to do with confidence and business. In this high-pressured world where we are available 24-7 through our computers and smartphones, we forget that business is all about managing relationships. Whether that involves our home lives, so we feel secure or grounded enough to stride out into the world, or feel confident enough to make new business connections and find new clients.

Confidence begins when you examine your behaviours and how you interact with people. Remember the girl I described who walked along, looking at the pavement? It took me deciding that I was going to start looking up, to change things. It wasn't anyone else coming and waving a magic wand. It had to come from me. It didn't cure my shyness overnight or make me ultra- confident, and yes, I still get scared. But no, standing up in front of a conference hall filled with people, holding a microphone to speak, doesn't scare me at all. I can't promise you'll ever feel that way, but I can give you some tricks that will make you more comfortable in giving it a go.

Now you know that confidence comes from accepting our flaws, and trying to fix things ourselves. I want you to think of what you can work on to make yourself appear more confident to the outside world. It's easier if we start by thinking about what makes someone appear confident.

Challenge 2

When we see people who are confident, they walk into a room with their shoulders back and, heads held up. They make eye contact with others in the room. They smile and shake hands with people they meet. And most of all, they listen and give other people their attention. A confident person is someone you want to hang around with.

For this challenge, I want you to make a list of three confident people you admire. They might be someone you know personally, a business owner, or celebrity who you admire. Note all of the characteristics that you believe make them confident. It might be the way they hold themselves in their body language or the way they dress and come across in interviews. Write down as much detail as possible. If something seems silly to you, still write it down. I want you to examine them as if they were right in front of you.

Take a look at that list. Are there similarities between those three individuals? Are there some things that you would like to be able to do – a firm handshake, eye contact or dressing well? Circle three things that you can work on. You might not be able to do them all yourself, but you can find help to achieve them. If it is a firm handshake, practice with a friend. These might feel like insignificant changes. Trust me when I say that these are the building blocks of confidence building. When we meet someone new, it takes a few seconds for him or her to form an opinion of us. Good posture, a firm handshake, and eye contact can help turn that into a good impression. When you choose someone to do business with or invest in, you want to feel that you are in safe, confident hands — understanding what we see and trust as confident traits help us to develop more them ourselves.

Confidence can be learned. Amy Cuddy, the social psychologist, has shown that our body language affects not only how others perceive us but also how but also how it affects our biochemistry.

Amy Cuddy experimented with a group of interviewees. She split the group into two, telling one group to carry on as they would before an interview and taking the others to one side. The first group (we'll call them group A) sat as they would, waiting for an interview. They hunched over their smartphones, or else brought their shoulders forward, cracked their arms and tried to make contact with the other interviewees who were all applying for the same job. The second group (we'll call them group B) then were taught the Wonder Woman pose. Whenever she appeared in her superhero outfit she would stand with her feet hip-width apart, shoulders back, head held up and her hands firmly on her hips. It was a strong and powerful pose, and every little girl in the 1980s wanted to be her.

What is interesting about this pose, Amy Cuddy and her team found, is that standing like Wonder Woman for two minutes changes your body chemistry. The stress hormone cortisol decreased and male testosterone increase, which tricks your body into believing it is confident.

Group A and B then went through the interview. The interview itself was made to be as stressful as possible with the interviewers not giving anything away or encouraging them. They sat stone-faced on a panel to make the interviewee as uncomfortable as possible. They had checked all of the applicants' hormonal and stress levels before and afterwards. Group A who sat hunched over with shut down body language increased their stress levels, whereas group B not only reduced them but they became more confident in doing so. The interviewees were then asked which applicants they would hire based solely on how they felt about how they performed in the interview. They chose everyone from group B.

If standing somewhere quiet for two minutes in the Wonder

Woman pose can have such a dramatic effect not only on your own body's chemistry but how others perceive you, this is a simple, invaluable tool to add to your confidence toolbox.

Every time I deliver a lecture or have to go on live television (believe me when I say that it's still scary!) I stand in the wonder woman pose in the toilets for two minutes. It might not be the most glamorous location, but those two minutes alone in that pose telling myself I can do it has had the most dramatic effect on my confidence building abilities. It might be unsustainable to stand like Wonder Woman all day long but having this pose to hand before a stressful situation works, well, wonders! I use it before networking events too.

We are creatures with hormones that tell us if we are scared, happy, in love or confident. It can only be a positive thing to be able to have some control over them, primarily when it doesn't involve a drug intervention, just a belief in our abilities and the power of the Wonder Woman pose.

The other body chemistry trick I learned from standing on the stage to perform musicals. I attended a stage school from the age of 11 to 15. I can't say I enjoyed the experience. I was teased for being too tall, too shy, too quiet, etc. What it did teach me was that I could face up to my fears and force myself into difficult situations and survive. Now I'm not suggesting that you need to put yourself on the stage or book yourself as a speaker for a large conference, but there are small ways we can test out boundaries now, and we always learn something from it, no matter how small.

What I learned from being made to stand on stage after stage and sing my heart out is that we all feel those sickening nervous butterflies in the stomach. Even the most confident girl at school still suffered from stage fright. I used to have it so bad that I would throw up in the toilets before going on stage, which was beginning to turn into a miserable existence, and I knew that I didn't want to keep feeling this way every time I had to go on stage.

Sickly butterfly feelings would come to me and also to those confident girls. Sure, they felt them, as they were a chemical reaction to being put into a stressful situation. The difference was that the confident girls wouldn't acknowledge them and go onto the stage. By allowing those feelings to come and not take over them, those butterflies only lasted for a few seconds. Then they were able to go onto the stage and perform.

By feeling these butterflies, we can acknowledge that they will pass, and not take over our performance. By doing that the cortisol levels reduce and those feelings fade away. If we tell ourselves that we are nervous, it becomes a vicious circle, and in the worst cases, you find yourself like I did -throwing up in the toilets. If we can convince ourselves that it is perfectly natural to have those feelings, (it is it is our body telling us that we are about to enter a stressful situation), then we can allow them to come and go. Thank your body for wanting to protect you, but that you've got it and The Wonder Woman pose is going to get you through this stressful situation.

Confidence is a balance of belief and body chemistry. It is as simple as that. Of course, it takes work, but there isn't anything magical we need to have or a complicated way of doing preparation, etc. Some people grow that confidence. We all come into the world as human beings ready to be influenced by our environment and outside experiences. The key is not to let them get the better of us.

I didn't have the best start in life with my father leaving when I was four, and my mother dying of breast cancer when I was nine. I refused to let these experiences define my future. Life can have horrible moments and people have lived through brutal and terrifying atrocities that I can't possibly imagine, *and I'm not for one moment comparing my life to theirs, or yours.*

We all have had experiences that have scared or hurt us. They can knock our confidence or change the way we see the world. Those are perfectly natural responses to have; it is what we do next with them that are important. We can get therapy, we can attend public speaking classes, and we can practice holding ourselves straight and not looking at the pavement anymore. We always have choices. Even when it can feel so dark and frightening out there in the big wide world as we build our freelance careers, we can still choose how we respond to rejections and feedback. I know that you can fix things as you go along, and if a shy orphan can stand up in front of hundreds of people and not want to hide in the bathroom, I know that you can do it too.

We've looked at the chemistry and body language of confidence; now I want us to look at practical ways we can make ourselves appear more confident when we are going out into the world to sell our art, products or services.

Each one of us has a goal or dream that we are striving towards. Some of us might have several things that we want to achieve. Having a clear goal is the only way we can move forward. Without a clear goal we don't know what to aim for, and more importantly, others don't know how to help us achieve something. If you don't have a goal to strive for, you spend your time lost or else trying lots of things hoping that the next one will be the right one. How exhausting!

There will be moments in our lives when we don't know what we want to do or what to aim for. That is perfectly natural. But I bet there are things that you are good at, or love doing, things that you are happy to spend lots of time on. I'm someone who enjoys lots of things. When I began my career in the 1990s, it was very unusual for someone to build a career in many different subjects. I was regularly being advised to choose one thing and focus on it. For a while, I did and picked photography. I would go home after working and take a class in textiles, writing or even trapeze. I realised very quickly that I would never be happy doing one thing. It was called Jack of All Trades then, and I'm glad that it has a new title: Portfolio career, although I'd prefer to call it a multi-faceted career.

You might be one of the lucky ones who have one passion and knows what they want to do. I admire these people as they can focus all of their drive and energy into one thing. I know that doesn't work for me, and although it might take my career on a wibbly, wobbly path with highs and lows, I wouldn't have it any other way.

Enough about me, let's get back to those goals. Part of our confidence toolbox is to know what we want to put in it. There is no point preparing for someone else's dream only finding out halfway through that we are miserable and unable to move forward. Sometimes parents, friends, and family offer suggestions of careers and goals to help us on our way. They may be afraid for us when they see us choose a creative path, which they think, will be a tough and challenging route.

I'm not suggesting that you pack in your safe job to jump off the cliff into the creative life you dream about. We still need to prepare a parachute for the way down; some snacks to eat on the way and a pot of gold to land in at the end would be nice to have as well. Goal setting can help us to have a dream, and that dream we can then prepare for so that it is sustainable and we can comfortably live in it. What we don't want to happen is that our dream turns into a nightmare. That is depressing, not only you but also for the people who care about you. This journey is about us making sure we plan for the dream and deal with problems that might get in our way.

What we don't want to do is to jump off into the unknown. That is as bad as having no goal at all.

Challenge 3

Challenge 3 is to set yourself a goal. Write down a goal you want to achieve in the next three to six months. Make it a realistic goal. Getting your website set up in a month might be possible if you are a computer whizz, but maybe writing all the copy of your new exhibition and getting the printed material ordered is a more realistic goal for you now. Choose something that you would feel proud of if you achieved it, but also make it something that you know is possible to accomplish in the month's time frame we have.

Sit down somewhere and use a pen and paper to write down what your goal is. Writing with a pen and paper activates a different part of our brain. (Plus if you are like me, I type faster than I think, so it is good to slow down with a pen when I am trying to let my thoughts flow). Write what your goal is at the top of the page. Sit for a moment and picture yourself achieving it. Be honest with yourself. No one else is going to read this.

- Write down when you want this to happen.
- What effect will this have on your future when you achieve it?
- Who do you need to help you achieve this?
- Is there anything else that you need to make this happen?
- How will you feel when you achieve it?

Now that you have your goal we need to work out how to help you achieve it. Look back at what you have written and make a list of all the people that you need to help you achieve this goal. Next, to the names write down what it is that you need them to do to help you and whether you need to pay them for their help or not. Next look at the timeframe you have set yourself. If it is a month add it to the calendar marking out each day you have left to work on it.

Have a look at all of the tasks that you will need to do to achieve your goal. Take each of these tasks and put them into an order of when each one needs to happen. Now plot each of those tasks onto the calendar. Only when we can see what we need to do and how much time we have to do it in, can we know if we have set enough time to achieve our goal. Once we have plotted all of the tasks, add the people onto the calendar who can help you to accomplish each task; this gives you a clear idea of when you need help during the process, and how much notice you need to provide these individuals for them to make time to help you.

If you need to pay these individuals, plot out when you need to pay them and how much; this is the first step in planning to achieve your goal - now you need to take the steps towards it by working through each task on your calendar.

You will always have setbacks or things take longer than planned. By plotting out, we can prepare for those moments and take part of the panic away, which in turn helps us gain confidence in our abilities and helps us to achieve our goals.

I always say, *"it is better to plan, then to panic."*

Once we are clear about our goal and the steps we need to achieve it, we can look at the third way of developing our confidence.

In today's electronic world even if we are a fine artist working in the studio a million miles from anywhere, at some point, we will have to use a computer to send emails, build a website and find new clients and customers.

Although we often go out into the world and present ourselves in person, there will be times when we are applying for funding, making new contacts for a career or negotiating a new job/client and we have to do it through email. Whether we love or hate email, it has become part of daily life. How we present ourselves in an email (or even in a letter) lets the other person know how confident we are in our self, and what we are selling.

Certain words can have a detrimental effect on your career when you use them regularly in correspondence. To help with some of them, people have even designed apps that will scan your emails for the offending words and highlight them. I prefer the old-fashioned way of retraining yourself not to use them. So what are these words, and why can they have a detrimental effect on my career?

The first one I want to talk about is the most overused, especially in the UK. In the UK if someone steps on your foot you would be the person to say sorry. *Yes, they stepped on you, and you say sorry!* When I say this to my students in places like Brazil and Turkey they think we must be crazy. Why on earth would you apologise when someone else has caused you pain? We also say sorry if we bump into someone, want to pass someone on the street or fumble to get change out of our pockets. It's as if we are sorry for everything. We also say sorry in person, on the telephone and in emails.

In a study of office workers, women who apologised more often were overlooked for promotion. They appeared unsure or unconfident in their work and the tasks they had to complete. Sorry is a powerful word.

I want you to look back at the last email you sent out to someone in connection with your career. Have a look through it and circle the word 'sorry.' How many times have you used it? Have you used it in every email? Is it the way you begin your correspondence to a new connection? Don't feel embarrassed if it is; you are not alone.

When I was starting as a photojournalist and trying to get meetings with picture editors to look at my portfolio, I sent out hundreds of emails. I made sure I found out who the picture editor was by name and wrote directly to them. I researched if the publication was a right fit for my work and I made sure to mention if we had a mutual connection or if I had been to an exhibition they admired. I had done my homework.

What I did next still makes me cringe. I began nearly every email with "*Sorry to bother you,*" or "*Sorry to email out of the blue*" etc. It might not seem so bad looking at these now, but those sorrys made me appear less confident to those picture editors. I was apologising for taking their time up, for popping up in their busy inbox. What I should have been conveying is that I was an exciting new contact/talent for them to meet and that they might be interested in featuring my work in their publication.

You might have thought this wasn't the end of the world, but when I removed these 'sorrys' and sent the emails out again, every picture editor replied to me. Did I learn a valuable lesson? Yes, I did, but it took me quite a while to get out of the habit of populating my letters and emails with sorrys. I had to come up with some key phrases that I could use instead and keep them to hand when I was writing.

Sorry is a powerful word. It should be used when you mean it. And if you mean it, then I hope you will say it in person rather than in an email or text message. I want you to reclaim sorry for when you are sorry and remember to use it with respect.

Here are some of the opening phrases that I use instead of ones beginning with sorry:

"*I'm getting back in touch to see whether you have had time to read the proposal I sent last week.*"

Rather than

"*I'm sorry to bother you when I know you must be very busy. I sent a proposal last week and wondered if you had had a chance to look at it.*"

The first one reads like someone who knows why they are getting in touch and is confidently checking in to see if they have understood what they sent.

The second one is rather grovelling. It reads like someone who is concerned about putting themselves forward and doesn't want to take up too much of someone's time. It reads not as an equal, but as someone who isn't sure.

When we put ourselves out into the world, we want to present the best image of ourselves, especially if we work in the creative industries. Often our talent is connected to ourselves as a package. We can't hide behind our work, as people now want to meet the artist, architect, photographer or designer behind the work. Even if we aren't feeling as confident as we could be, we need to show the world that we are confident in our abilities and our talents. If we don't believe in our work, no one else is going to.

"Sorry I was late to the conference, and I missed the beginning of the meeting."

"Can we have a catch up for the section I missed at the beginning of the meeting?"

I believe that we shouldn't say sorry for being late in an email. (Go ahead and still say it in person, as that is good manners and manners I believe are a good thing.) Not saying sorry in an email is a tough thing to do. I mentioned manners, and you might feel that it is rude not to say sorry, but bear with me while I explain why you shouldn't do it.

If you are late for something, that other person already knows you were late. The time has passed. You probably said sorry in person when you arrived at the meeting; they don't need to hear it again. What you are writing to them about isn't being late; it is for the information you missed. That is the real focus of this email. Leave the sorry to one side and get to the point.

We all have busy lives and spending the first part of correspondence apologising for something you can't fix or is in the past, and you have already apologised in person for it, is a waste of time and immediately places you in an unequal position. Get to the point of why you are writing that email and leave the sorry for when you are face to face.

The second word I want us to eliminate is the word *just*. Go back to those emails again and see how many times you use the word.

"I'm just checking in..."
"I'm just wondering if..."
"I'm just getting in touch to say..."

Just is one of those words that negatively impact on the way others perceive you. The word just suggests that you aren't sure or else you aren't valuing yourself.

Keeping emails brief and to the point helps everyone. People don't want to read long wordy emails- they don't have the time. You can still be polite without coming across as unconfident. You need to stop apologising but also look for words that can make you come across as aggressive or critical too.

- Sorry
- Just
- Hopefully
- But
- Try
- Actually

Language is often the first way that we communicate what our business/talent is with the outside world. It's vital that we are presenting the best version of ourselves at all times. We don't need to fear how we come across in our correspondence; it's a good idea to do a check now and then to make sure we are coming across as professional, confident and enthusiastic about the work we are doing. Be proud of what you are creating and make others feel excited to be part of your journey.

Now our confidence toolbox has some things that we can use and practice. New habits take time and determination. You will have days when you don't feel confident at all, but having a series of tools to help you, like the Wonder Woman pose.

Practice makes perfect or at least improves on what you already have. If you send an email that still contains the negative words, don't give yourself a hard time. Pause for a moment and know that you can try again another time. I still catch myself putting in the odd just or but, and now make sure I read through everything before I press send. I know you'll get there too.

2

Values

When we begin our creative careers and businesses, we are excited about what the future holds and what paths we will take. We share our excitement with friends and dream big about what we want to do. Being able to communicate what our 'mission' is, is one of the most important things you can do for your business.

We set off on our path, and we have thoughts and feelings about how we want to run our business. Maybe you have an eco ethos and want to use local manufacturing, or perhaps you want to share the story behind your artwork as part of the package. All of this can be summed up as values.

Values are the parts of our business that we feel strongly about and are the vision of how we want to do things, design things or care for our employees and customers. Even if you are a solo artist/designer, you will still have a set of values that you care passionately about and want to share.

I want you to start by thinking about your own personal values. Put all thoughts of your creative career to one side for the moment. Think about how you choose to live your life. Maybe you live in the centre of a bustling city, or somewhere quiet in the countryside, or perhaps you live with your parents and dream of owning your own home one-day, or you share an apartment with flatmates and love the creative interactions that you have each day. How we choose to live our own lives is based on our values.

I'm a vegetarian and have been for over half of my existence. I can't imagine eating meat again, so for now being vegetarian is one of the values that form my life. I also recycle and use non-chemical beauty products. I wouldn't describe myself as a hippie, as the stereotype of a hippie doesn't fit with my value system. By defining a few fundamental values of how I live my life, I might be helping you build up a picture of the type of person I am.

I want you to write out a list of all of the things that you believe are values you stand by to create the life you have or want to have. They might be the way you consume products, i.e. chemical free, they might be the way you structure your day with meditation or dance practice. Alternatively, they might be the way you interact with others with kindness and assistance. Write down every value you wouldn't want to live without; these are the things that make you the person you are or want to be.

Take a look at that list. If you handed it to a friend, do you think they would recognise it as you? Are there some values on there that you hope to develop in the future but haven't implemented into your life yet? We can call these *Aspirational Values*. I know that I would like to make time to build exercise into my life so that I feel fitter and stronger. It isn't something I have done yet, but I'm working on it.

Values are things that we develop over time. They can be fluid and change as we grow. Through education, experience and influence we change our values and how we want to live our life. It is the same for your business/career.

When I was starting, it was unusual for people to talk about green issues or the carbon footprint we were creating by getting on flights or consuming electronic devices and clothing. Now it's a commonplace for people to talk about recycling – whether at home or work, and we are more conscious about what we consume and how we dispose of it. Values change. However, with change comes consequence. Some changes we have no control over, they might be due to conflict or war, economics, government policies or new technology. Sometimes they might be changes that happen abroad rather than in our own country, and they can impact how we can run our business.

Values are, and we shouldn't fear them changing. It is how we stand by them and communicate them to our clients and customers that matters.

How do we find values for our business and career? Are they different to the values we mould our personal life around? I used to do bookbinding and used leather covers for my work. Some may feel that this went against my values of being a vegetarian. It would depend on my reasoning for being a vegetarian, which was for health and didn't stop me caring for animals, and I would source leathers that had come from a tannery that I trusted. It meant that I didn't tell my customers I was vegetarian, as the words vegetarian and leather worker don't go well together. I kept my value system and decided how I communicated it to my customers and clients.

When we are solo entrepreneurs, artists and creatives, our personal values are often closely tied to our business values. If they weren't, it would be tough to go out into the world and sell our products and services as we wouldn't believe in what we were doing or care about what we were putting out into the world.

For this next stage, I want to help you to find out what your business/career values are. Without understanding what these values are you won't be able to design how you run your business or plan for growth.

As we form the foundation of our business and careers, we need to make sure we are presenting a real and honest version of how we want our business to be. When we set out to do something that goes against our values, we can feel uncomfortable, frustrated, angry or scared. Not staying true to our values is an awkward place to be.

Make a list of all the *personal values* you want to change at the moment. These are the things that you feel intimately connected with, like being vegetarian or recycling at home.

Next, make a list of all the values that you would like to bring into your business/career. (This is for your *dream* business/career-think big!) These could be things like a duvet-day for all your staff, or sourcing all of your materials from your home country. We can call these *Aspirational Values*.

When we are new and trying to make a name for ourselves, we might say yes to products or opportunities, which don't wholly sit with our value system. We may do this for the money, or because that product will help us achieve something in the future. Sometimes we have to do things for the money, but I want you to think about how you would feel if you took jobs and clients only for the money. Would you feel fulfilled, passionate and excited about your work? I have a feeling that the spark that first got you excited about making a creative career would go out.

When I was building my photographic career, I used to do weddings on the side. Wedding photographers and documentary photographers can have a problematic relationship. At the core of the photojournalism group that I socialised with and worked with in London, it was a value that documentary photography was more valuable than wedding photography. Some of those photographers looked down on ones who took wedding photography jobs at the weekend. Sometimes we had bills to pay or had invoices to collect, and a weekend wedding fee seemed like the perfect way to bring in a lump sum. To sit with my photographic values, I only took weddings that would allow me to shoot in a documentary style with informal portraits and group shots. I enjoyed the work and being part of someone's special day.

When I began to take on more wedding work only for the money, something changed. I found myself clock watching or getting bored hearing the fourth best man's speech that month using the same jokes as the previous wedding. That was when I knew my values were no longer being honoured so I decided to make a change. I went back to shooting only documentary work and became a much pleasanter person to be around. I know lots of wedding photographers who love every minute of it. I admire their work and see that they are staying true to their values.

I don't know if you have ever been served in a shop, or by a member of waiting staff who doesn't want to be there? You can tell that they are clock watching or see you as an inconvenient part of their day. No smiles, no polite hellos are exchanged. Instead, you get a cold delivery of your order, and the plate slapped down on the table. The grumpy member of staff has ruined that treat of a coffee or going out for your anniversary meal. When we stop enjoying doing something, it isn't only ourselves who feel it. Everyone else around us does.

Values can make or break your day. Working out which ones are yours can be the difference between having a career you love or hate. Once we have a set of values we want to shape our business with, we can work out how we communicate them with our clients and customers. Take a look back at the personal values that you wrote down. Are there any that you would also like to form the basis of your business/career? Look at the business values that you discovered from doing the exercise. Write a sentence that describes each of those values and why they are essential for your future business/career.

The exercise will help you to begin writing your *'mission statement,'* which you can use to communicate your business, product, artwork and talent to the outside world. Have a look at people or companies that you admire. They don't have to be in the same field as you. You might admire someone like a fashion designer or food company. Think about what it is that you admire about them. What was it that drew you to their product or service? What made you go back again and again and purchase from them? Maybe you haven't bought anything from them, but you want to in the future.

The way companies present themselves can tell us what their values are or how they want us to perceive them. Write a list of reasons why you have or want to use their product or service. Write a list of what drew you to them. Was it their design, ease of use or the fantastic customer service they provided?

By looking at all of these elements, you can begin to form a picture of what you love about them and relate it to your business/ career.

Thinking about your business/ or future career now, how would you like your customers and clients to see you? What will you do to show them your values? Look at your list of *aspirational values*. How will you achieve them in the future? Can you aim to complete one of them in the next year? Write down what help you would need to make that happen. Do you need new skills, a piece of software, some investment or more time?

Values are the foundation of our business and career. We need to be clear about what they are and how we communicate them. If our values do have to change, we need to accept the consequences of that change. How would you find new ones or restructure the old ones? We might lose some along the way.

We can communicate what our values are, not only in a mission statement, pitches, and our presentations but also in our marketing, publicity and branding.

Think of 10 words that represent your values. You can build them into your *mission statement*, website copy and pitches.

Having a bank of words that represent who you are and what you stand for can help you to communicate your message efficiently with new clients and customers. It can also help you make sure you are creating the *dream career* that you want.

3

Customer Profiling

lthough you may work as a solo freelancer or sell your
services or products directly to business, you will still find
customer profiling invaluable. Customer profiling is easy to
do and can save you money on marketing your products or services.

In our lifetime we have all been customers. We know what it feels
like to enter a shop or join a queue at the cinema. We understand
the process of asking for something, choosing what we want and
exchanging money for that product or service. We probably have
a favourite place we like to shop or a cafe that we like to visit with
our friends. Before we dive into customer profiling for your business/
career, I want to ask you to take a moment to think about yourself
as a customer.

I want you to spend this week taking note of every time you are
a customer. Note down where you are, if the experience was a good
or bad one and why. Also note down if there was a physical person
who took the money from you, or if the system was automated online
or at a self-service till. Make sure you note down which day it was,
and the time, this is going to become valuable information for you.

Once you have done that look at what you have written, were
there regular times that you bought something? Did you return to the

26

same places again and again? If so, why did you do that, and were all of your customer experiences positive? If not, why not, and what made an experience a positive one?

Sometimes I can be a creature of habit. I like to go to the same coffee shop to work in. The baristas know me by name; they know how I want to have my coffee and allow me to sit for a few hours before the lunchtime rush. I feel relaxed in the café, I need noise to work in, and I purchase several coffees and the odd slice of cake in exchange for renting that table and seat, for me, this is positive customer experience. My husband needs silence to work. He can cope with one cup of coffee and a chat, but this environment isn't right for him to work in. He enjoys the café and uses it in a completely different way to me. We both have a positive customer experience but for very different reasons.

Now that we understand and have documented the experience of being a customer ourselves, I will explain what customer profiling is.

Customer profiling is one of the most powerful marketing tools you can have. It isn't complicated to do, and often you can ask your customers themselves to get the information you need. Customer profiling is all about putting yourself into the shoes of the customer. You begin to understand what they do with their day, whether they have hobbies or interests and whether they go on holiday or work seven days a week. Although this might sound like very basic information, it is what you do with this information that is important.

Start by looking at the basic customer profiling set of questions. These are the things that you would want to find out about your customer.

- Age Gender
- Wage/Salary
- Rental or Home Owner

- How do they get to work? Car/bus/bike/train/walk
- Are they married/in a partnership/divorced/widowed?
- Do they have children?
- Do they have a hobby? What/when/how often?
- Do they go to the gym?
- Do they go on holiday? Where/when/how/cost etc.?

You can make your profile as simple or as in-depth as you like. It all depends on how much information you want. You might be wondering what to do with this information and why do you need it?

At some point in your business/career, you are going to want to have a client or customer make a purchase from you for a product or service. If this doesn't ever happen then we have no business or career, we have a hobby. I want you to make a thriving career in the creative industries so at some point money will have to be exchanged for your product or service. What we don't want to do is waste money on advertising and marketing to the wrong clients or customers.

If we try to speak to everyone, we end up speaking to no one.

A scattergun approach to your advertising/marketing not only wastes money, but it can also damage your brand/reputation. You wouldn't want to advertise your bespoke fashion line at a discount clothing store, and you wouldn't want to offer your one on one dance training to a community that can't afford it. Customer profiling helps you to identify the right customers for your product or service, and in turn that enables you to work out the best way to communicate with them so that they want to purchase from you again and again.

We know that we have all been customers ourselves, but we may not be our 'own' customers. We need to work out who our customers are.

When I was starting as a creative business coach, I wasn't sure who my clients and customers were. I thought that they were all going to be start-ups or university graduates. By going out and questioning that group, I discovered that although they were interested in what I was doing, they wouldn't purchase from me until their business was up and running.

Through another set of customer profiling I discovered that my ideal customer was in their late 20s to late 30s, and I had a second and third customer as well, someone who had been in business a while and was looking to grow their business to the next level, and someone who was looking to take a career side-step. This third customer was in their late 40's to 50's.

You might find that you have more than one customer as well. Don't be disheartened if you do. It means that you have to tailor your marketing and advertising to those two customers in a different way. By doing that your message will be stronger, and they will be more likely to purchase from you.

When you have asked your potential customers the profiling questions (and add more of your own) look back through all of the answers. Can you work out what they do each day, how they get to work and whether they go to the same places each week? Break that information down even further. Do they take the train to work? What do they see on that train journey? Are there advertising posters on the train? Do they pass a billboard along the train track? Do they buy a cup of coffee on the train? Does the coffee come in a printed cup? Is there advertising on it? Was it purchased from the buffet car or did someone wheel trolley to their table? Was there advertising space on that trolley? Did they listen to the radio to pass the time? Were adverts playing between the songs?

Is this beginning to help you build up a picture of all the times during their day that you could use for a marketing or advertising opportunity? It might make you uncomfortable doing this and you might feel a bit like *'Big Brother'* watching their every move. Think about it a different way. Your products/service will make these people's lives better. Your artwork will inspire them or brighten their day. Your service will help them with a problem they have been having in their lives. Everything that you have to offer will be of use to someone in the world.

Money is only part of the exchange. It is your knowledge, talent or inspiration that you are selling. If you don't go out and offer it up to your customers and clients, you are doing them a disservice by keeping it to yourself. Being able to communicate with them, in the right way and at the right time allows you to tell them what you have to offer and how it can help/change their lives. Customer profiling is the shortcut to being able to do that successfully. There is nothing creepy about it, as long as we are doing it for good, rather than evil purposes.

Once you understand the way your customer or client feels that day, you can plan how to approach them. I should mention here that you might not have an individual client or customer if you sell business to business. You might be a documentary maker who sells their work to a TV channel, or a software designer who sells to corporate companies. Although you are a business selling to another business, there will still be another human involved in the chain of purchasing. There will be one person that you deal with, send emails to and eventually submit an invoice. For example, if it is a TV channel, you will be approaching the Programme Commissioner. When you do the customer profiling exercise, keep this person in mind. It is them that you will be directing your advertising and marketing to. Think about the problems they are trying to solve.

Take another look at the customer profiling answers that you have for your clients/customers. Make a list of all the opportunities you have to advertise or market to them.

Customer profiling is easy to do, and often it is free. You can either imagine your customer and client or set up a free survey on a platform like SurveyMonkey. By directly asking your customer/client you may get insights and information that you hadn't thought about as you may not be your customer. Over time the habits and type of customer you want/need may change. It is useful to repeat the customer profiling exercise every year. If we don't remember to innovate and develop our business/career, we can get left behind. Technology, communication, and peoples want and need change over time.

A decade ago we didn't have smartphones, now 86% of people check their emails or visit websites from their phone and this is increasing every year. We need to make sure that the way we communicate with our customers fits these new ways and technology. Check that your website opens on mobile phones. Make sure the text and images are at a size that you can read.

It doesn't mean that analogue ways of marketing and advertising (like leaflets) don't work. You need to make sure you have thought and researched where to use them.

When I was selling one of my courses, I knew that it was for mothers starting their own creative business now that the children had reached school age. I knew that they regularly went out for coffee with their girlfriends when they dropped the kids off at school. I also knew that the customers I wanted to attract for the course were creatives, and had some disposable income. This information not only helped me to helped me to narrow down the type of coffee shop I wanted to leave my leaflets in but also which area, which city and where to hold my course/workshops.

If I had put my leaflets in any old coffee shops across the city, not only would it have cost me more money to print extra leaflets, they wouldn't have reached the right customers. They might have been interested in my course/workshop but unable to afford it, or else it wasn't the right time for them to take the course as their children were still in kindergarten. Being very specific about how and when you target your customers and clients can be the difference between no sale or a sale and a regular client. I know which I prefer.

Customer profiling is one part of the toolbox. How you use that information and share it with them needs to be carefully considered, not only in the content, language but also in the technology that you use to deliver the message. Start to keep a folder of marketing and advertising campaigns that you are inspired by. They might not be for something that you use, but something about them stood out for you or made you look twice. By examining other campaigns and ways of marketing, we can learn what might work for our own business. Have fun with it. Be what you do best - *be creative.*

4

Personal Finance

For us to have a sustainable career or business, we need to think about money. Money can be a word that makes most creatives wince at the thought of it. We spend so much time making our artwork, products or services that when it comes to the money, we often leave it as an afterthought. I want this to change.

When I was starting, I found it hard to price myself accurately. I wasn't sure if I should ask for an overall job price or an hourly rate. As I moved through my career, this question didn't go away. I looked at what others were charging and often thought it wasn't enough. It left me feeling stressed, hassled and nervous about sending an invoice. I wanted to let you know that it doesn't have to be this way. I might even make you think about money as something more than a way to be paid for your work. More about that later.

I want us to start right back at the very beginning with money. As a child, I had 20p (about 15 cents) per week pocket money to go and buy sweets from the shop over the road. I would spend the lot and devour all of the sweets over the course of the day. My older brother would also spend all of the money, but he would make the sweets last for the whole week until pocket money day came round again. I was in awe of his willpower and the fact that he could plan to make sure he had sweets every day. I learned a valuable lesson from him. Even though we had the same amount of money and could choose from the same selection of sweets, my brother had worked out a way to make every day a sweet day, and I want you to start looking at your finances in the same way.

When we create something and put it out into the world, we can do it for a number of reasons. We can share it to give others pleasure, we can share it to make a statement, we can share it to attract new customers and clients, and at some point, we will share something to generate an income. As we start with our new business or career, there will be times when we have to give our skills/knowledge/time away for free. What I want you to start thinking is that nothing is for free. Even if money isn't exchanged, there must be some reward for what you have done. The reward could be in the form of new contacts in an industry you have been trying to work in; it could be a way of learning new skills from an expert or a way of growing your audience in the run-up to them making a purchase. What we mustn't find ourselves doing is continually giving away our time, knowledge and skills for no rewards. There has to come a time when you received payment with money and value your own time/skills enough to accept payment for them.

So how on earth do we work out what to charge for our skills, product or services? It all begins with knowing what we need. I want you to think about the life that you have right now. Think about how you spend your days. Do you take friends out for coffee; go to the cinema at the weekend or order takeaways? Maybe you go to the theatre or watch a dance performance, or you save your money and stay home watching box sets.

Think back to the goal that you wanted to achieve when you started reading this book. Have a look at what you wanted to achieve not only in the next 2-3 months but how you want your career to look in five years. (I am assuming that it is going to be different from how you are living your life right now). You might be in rented accommodation and dream of owning your own home, or you are working out of your bedroom and want to have your own studio. These are all positive goals to aim for; the only thing we need to achieve them is a focus, time and money.

I often wonder why as creatives we have such a tormented relationship with money? Countless times I have heard my creative students tell me that they are no good with money, that it frightens them, or that they have no idea how to start or manage it. I used to feel this way too. After getting over the fact that math isn't so awful, I am confident in my pricing, and I want you to be also. I am going to help you work out a system that works best for you and allows you to aim for those goals and help you work out ways to achieve them.

The first thing that we need to do is to work out what we need personally as a human being to survive from day to day. There is no complicated formula for doing this. We only need to add up the data and look at is the figures that come out at the other end. Nothing too scary.

Start with a basic spreadsheet. If the thought of that panics you, you can make a list on a piece of paper and have a calculator to hand. Start with five columns. In one list the items, in two the daily total, in three the weekly total, in the fourth the monthly total, and the fifth the yearly total. Don't worry about what those totals will be now; start with column one.

In the first column list everything that you personally buy or pay for in a year; this isn't anything to do with your business now; this is only you personally as a human being. Start by listing everything that you buy or pay for in a year. We need to make sure that we haven't forgotten anything. You might have children or pets as well. If you are the sole carer for them make sure you add them to the list in terms of school fees, clothes, food, classes, etc. If you share the costs with a partner, add the items to the list and divide the cost by 50%.

Once you have your list of items, we are now going to look at any other money that comes to you over the course of a year.

You might be lucky enough to own another property that generates you an income, or your partner/parents give you an allowance. Any other income that is personal to you adds to the bottom of that list under income. Remember that this is only personal income now and nothing to do with your career or business.

The next part will need you to find out the figures for them. Look at every item on that list and work out how much it costs you per year to have it. If you pay a weekly heating bill to warm your rented flat, multiply that bill by 52 weeks, this gives you the yearly total. In column 4 list all of the annual costs. Once you have them, work out the monthly cost and the weekly cost of that item. Have a look at the item list in column one again. Have you missed anything? Do you grab a coffee or a newspaper on the way to work, or do you meet up with friends on Friday night for a drink? All of those costs you need to add to this personal finance audit. I am a bit of a coffee addict, and I spend about three hours per day working in cafes. I work better with the noise of chatter and the hum of the coffee machine. For me to spend those three hours in the coffee shop, I purchase two coffees.

Each coffee I buy costs £2.50

Two coffees a day equals £2.50 x 2 = £5.00

In a week that's 7 X £5.00 = £35

In a month it's 4 X £35.00 = £140.00

Do you see where I'm going with this? Now for the shock- in a year I discovered that I spend *£1680 on coffee!* I was horrified when I first saw this figure. I began to think about what I could do each year with £1680, beach holidays I confess were my first thought. Are you starting to think about those 'little' things that you unconsciously spend money on each week?

Once I had got over the initial shock of the money I was spending on coffee, I thought about the benefits. I use the coffee shop as my nomadic office. I have a warm welcome when I enter, and the baristas know me by name. We always have interesting and inspiring conversations before I sit down to do my work. There are other regulars that I see every day. Sometimes they have jobs they want to put me forward for, and other times I recommend them to my clients. That £5 per day suddenly becomes an excellent value for money. It offers me a place to work, a place to network and makes new contacts. It inspires me and helps me to come up with new ideas, and it gives me a delicious cup of coffee. When we work alone it is so important to find other creatives to socialise and network with - that cup of coffee gives me all of that. I factor this into my yearly costs as much more than a refreshment break. It might mean I don't get that beach holiday, but it gives me more than a couple of weeks in the sun.

Have another look at all of the 'little' things that you spend money on. Are there some that you can do without, or like my coffee, are there things that bring you extra value and are worth keeping? Don't underestimate looking after your mental health when you build your career/business. As freelancers, we spend much time alone with our thoughts and ideas. If there are small things that bring you pleasure and energy to keep going, don't exclude them all. It does allow you to see where your money is going. If there is something you are saving up for, it shows you where you can make cutbacks. I could reduce my coffee intake to one a day and save £840 per year. That could be the difference between buying a new piece of equipment for my business or not. Remember to look back at those goods you are aiming for and decide what is more important to you.

Have another look at that list of items now and make sure you have added everything. There may be things that you remember later. That's fine. It isn't a fixed thing. It will change, grow and shrink as the year goes on, based on your habits. Make sure you have a look at it every month or every three months to check you haven't missed anything.

As well as the outgoings (money going out) and income (money coming in) I want you to think about *Contingencies*, or as I like to call it *Plan B*. We've all had those moments when we are living our day as usual, and then something comes along to surprise us. It might be a trip to the dentist, and we need to pay for a filling, or our car breaks down right when we needed it, so we have to pay garage bills and hire a car for the week. Life will always be filled with unexpected surprises, some good and some bad. We need to be prepared for the bad so that it doesn't have a detrimental affect on our personal lives and in turn, our business. You don't want to find yourself in the position of taking your marketing budget to pay the dentist.

Plan B doesn't need to be painful (unless you have a root canal) if you plan for it.

Those £5 per day coffees I didn't notice I was spending, and a plan B fund can both be handled in the same way. The suggested amount to put to one side is between 15 to 20% of the total amount you need to survive each week, month and year. If it costs you £200 per week to keep your lifestyle, you will need to put £40 per week into the Plan B fund, which might sound like a lot, but spreading it across each week will make it much easier to deal with than a huge surprise bill one month, which isn't complicated to do. We can't continue to be an ostrich and bury our head in the sand about money. Next week spend some time thinking about what you want from your life, and whether your finances will cover it now, or whether you need to make some changes. I don't want you to be afraid of those figures. Sure there will be shocks, like my coffee habit, and there will be items you hadn't realised were costing you so much. Isn't it better to know that now so that you can make plans for the rough times along the way?

Being honest with our spending habits and ourselves is the first step in getting a grip on our finances, not only in our personal lives but in our business as well. Money isn't an evil thing we have to fear. Money empowers us. It gives us choices, it allows us to change the life we are living, it helps us to give our children great opportunities, and it takes away the fear of not knowing how much we have left at the end of every month.

My older brother and his *sweet-saving-ways* are the way that I want you to think about your personal finance. You want to make sure you have enough money to last the whole week, and maybe some left over as well.

How is this making you feel about your finances at the moment? Fearful, embarrassed or excited? You don't have to be a math whizz to know how much money you have coming in and going out. If you are worried that it is too late to start, take heart that I used to feel that way also. All it took was a couple of days sitting down and going through everything, for a lifetime of not worrying about my bank balance. Taking control of your money will empower you. All you need is a simple spreadsheet or a list.

Once you have filled it all in and added your 15 or 20% for plan B, added any other income and inputted all of the data - you will come up with a weekly, monthly, yearly total of cost for your life. These figures are known as DRAWINGS. We'll need these figures as we move onto the next section about finance.

5

Cash Flow Forecasting and Bookkeeping

We know that every business and career needs money. If you are creating something and don't accept payment you only have a hobby. Hobbies are fun things to have, but they won't let us pay the rent or feed ourselves. I do silversmithing as a hobby. I know I am not going to make a career out of it, but it brings me pleasure, so I continue to do it. Hobbies can enrich our lives in other ways. I want you to think about ways you can enrich your career with money.

We have worked out what we need to have the lifestyle we are already living. I am hoping that you want to aim for more during the course of your career and the best way to achieve that is to plan for it financially.

When we decide that we want to earn a living from our talents, not only are we sharing our gifts with the world, we are also creating a life that makes us happy and fulfilled. You have already taken the brave step of deciding to create your path. That is a courageous thing to do. I want to help you make sure that you can continue along that path for many years to come. Creative industries shouldn't be poorly paid industries. We are part of a negative culture that often expects creatives to hand over their work and skills for free. I believe this needs to stop. We wouldn't enter the supermarket and fill up our basket for free. We wouldn't ask our accountant to do our accounts for nothing and wouldn't expect our landlord to give us our flat for free. Once you begin to respect your talents and skills in the same way, it will become easier to ask for money for them and not feel embarrassed about it.

The next part of the finance package that I want you to look at is the finance for your business/career. Sorting out the finance for your work doesn't have to be complicated or frightening. The first time I saw a cash flow forecasting spreadsheet I was terrified! It looked like such a daunting thing to get my head around. There were many columns that I needed to add data to and terms that I had never heard of before. I am determined that you won't have the same experience as me. I am going to break it down into small chunks for you so that you understand what each part means before we put it all back together again on a giant spreadsheet. Don't fear the spreadsheet! I promise to guide you through this in the least painful way possible.

I will start by explaining what cash flow forecasting is and why you need it even if you are a solo freelancer doing your tax returns. You might be thinking that cash flow forecasting is only for big business. It is such a useful tool for you to have right now and if there ever comes a time that you want to attract investors or speak to the bank manager, they will want to see your cash flow forecasting spreadsheet.

In its most basic form, a cash flow forecasting spreadsheet tells you what money comes into your business and what money goes out. I call it chasing the money.

A	B	C	D
ITEM	January	February	March
Opening bank balance	£2000	£1000	**-£1250**
Total *money coming in* – invoices etc.	£500	£750	£5000
Total spending *money out*	£1500	£3000	£2000
Closing bank balance	£1000	-£1250	£1750

In this mini spreadsheet, I have put some basic items in the first column A, including the opening bank balance, the total money that has come into the business from sales/invoices etc, the total money spent on the business (we call this money going out) and finally, the closing bank balance.

In column B we have all of those figures for the month of January. (In the UK the tax year usually begins and ends on April 5th, so you might want to start this column with April.)

We then take the closing bank balance for January and carry it up to column C and put it into the column for the opening bank balance. This month you might not have had much money coming in and have spent £3000 getting ready to prototype your product, frame your work for an exhibition or create a marketing campaign for your new service. This month we have a deficit of £1250. We carry this deficit into the opening bank accounts column from March. Don't panic at this moment that we are starting the month with a negative figure.

All that extra money we spent in February to create our new products, frameworks or marketing our service has paid off, and we have generated £5000 for our business. As we spent so much money last month, we don't need to spend as much this time, so we only spend £2000 on the business this month. Now that deficit has balanced out, and we have the closing bank balance of £1750, which we carry on over to April's opening bank balance and continue the process, it is as simple as that. What comes in and what goes out, and how much we spend on our career or business each month when it is broken down into its simple parts like this, it didn't feel so scary.

Creating your cash flow forecasting spreadsheet is only a matter if expanding those items in column A so that they appear in more detail. Precisely in the way, you worked out your personal finances, but this time the outgoings and income relate to your business *only*.

Your personal finance totals that we called DRAWINGS you add to your cash flow forecast spreadsheet. DRAWINGS are what you would *like* to draw from the business or as a wage. I say *like*, as you may not be able to take this full amount right now.

Let's go back to those DRAWINGS that you collected from doing the personal Finance audit. Work out what you would need to live on as a monthly wage and add this monthly figure to your spreadsheet. This figure is your first bit of data that you need to input. If you find that this changes over the year, go back to your personal finance audit sheet and adjust it, then come back to the forecasting sheet and correct it. Figures are fluid as life is. There will always be things we hadn't planned. We need to prepare for all extra costs along the way. *Money is like water; it flows in and out of our life. We need to be in control of the tap so that it doesn't all get washed away.*

You might be feeling overwhelmed by getting a grip on your finances, so I want to explain why cash flow forecasting is going to help your business/career. By knowing what is coming in and going out of your business at any one time, you can begin to see where there are gaps in income. You might always attend trade fairs in the autumn to sell to the Christmas market. Or you know that you have a large dance project coming up in the summer and there will be times when you are planning rather than working.

Those moments when we are creating or planning for something might not be giving us a weekly income, but they are still part of the costs we have to incur to build our career/project/business. Remember my two coffees a day in the café? Although I am doing work towards my business in that café, I'm not being paid to be there. In fact, it costs me £5 per day. I see that as an investment in my work; and although the work I am creating at the moment isn't earning me an income, in the future it will.

We know as freelance creatives that we can't draw an hourly income for every moment we work on our business. We don't have a boss, sick pay or have to commute. We decided to take the riskier path and create a life we would be happy living. It is why it is so essential for us to understand our finances as no one is going to look after our business/career, except us. I don't want that to frighten you, but we do need to be realistic about whether our talent and passion will give us enough to live on now and in the future.

While I built my career as a photojournalist in London, I would wait on tables until 2 am and then start my photojournalist work at 10 am, six days a week. There were days when I was exhausted, and I knew that I hadn't found enough clients or built my profile yet to leave my job waiting tables. I knew that it wouldn't be forever, and that kept me going on days when I had to deal with drunk customers or cycle home in the middle of the night. *Beginnings take time.* We are not all lucky enough to have parents or spouses to support us. If you do, be grateful every day for that amazing gift they have given you and make sure you work hard, and that you can offer someone else that same gift one day.

By filling in a cash flow forecast spreadsheet, you can see when you need some investment or where you need to make cutbacks. You can plan for those projects or take an evening job for a couple of months to pay off some debts. There is no wrong or right way to build a career. All you can do is make sure you have all of the facts in front of you so that you can make calculated decisions. Most new businesses fail because they don't have a handle on their finances. Cash flow forecasting helps you to keep one step ahead and know how much money you have to spend and more importantly, how much you need to save.

When I began my career as that waitressing photojournalist, I wasn't aware that newspapers could take two months to pay an invoice, no matter what payment terms you had written on your invoice. It meant that I couldn't rely on having that money land in my account for 60 days or more. Now imagine if every person I worked for did that. Suddenly you need to make sure you can afford to work for nothing for two months until the funds come in. If you need to take a second job while you build your career while working for someone else, there is no shame in that. It shows that you are making solid foundations before you leap to create your freelance career. The day you hand in your notice and go alone will feel sweeter as you are safe in the knowledge that you can afford to do so.

Cashflow forecasting will show you if you have enough money to cover your DRAWINGS (salary). You need to plan what to do if you can't cover your basic living costs from your business although you might want to panic if that happened! Remember I said before that it is better to plan than to panic. I want you to make sure each month that you have planned out your finances in the same way you would sit down to write your to-do list.

Financial planning doesn't need to be painful. Some fantastic online software packages can now help you with this. They link up to your bank account (in most cases) and create invoices, cash flow, forecasts and opening and closing monthly bank balances with the press of a button. In the same way, you would write a list, make time each month to sit down and input the data; it also makes it easier for an accountant to file your tax returns. Before I tackle the world of tax, I want us to have one last look at the cash flow forecasting sheet.

The cash flow forecasting sheet is split into monthly columns. At the top, you input all of the money that you have coming in from any sales or work that you do for your business. Next, put a section called 'cash out' and under this heading, list items that you have to pay to run your business or have your career. They will differ from person to person, just as a personal finance audit will look different from person to person. I split my items into sections that the UK government tax return site suggests. These are the nine headings:

1. Cost of goods bought for resale or goods used.
2. Car, van and travel expenses after private proportion use.
3. Wages, salaries, and other staff costs.
4. Rent, rates, power, and insurance costs.
5. Repairs and renewals of property and equipment.
6. Accountancy, legal and other professional fees.
7. Interest and bank and credit card etc. financial charges.
8. Telephone, fax, stationary and other office costs.
9. Other allowable business expenses (client entertaining costs are not an allowable expense).

These things change all of the time and differ from country to country. It is essential that you check with your own government office or helpline to make sure you aren't claiming for something you are not allowed or missing out on something you can claim for.

You can, of course, make your own headings. I believe it is always good to chat with an accountant when you are first setting up, even if you go on to file your own tax returns. They will help you to set up a system and inform you of what you can and can't claim for at that time. Remember to check for yearly accounting updates though. You might be missing out on things you can claim for, and accountants will keep up-to-date with that information.

Once you have decided on how you are going to layout your items into stationary, telephone calls etc., you can add them to your sheet in the same way you did for your personal finance audit. I put subsistence on here as well. Subsistence is only claimable when I am working away on business; It means I can claim for meals I ate while away. I pop this under my travelling expenses when I file my tax return. You used to be able to claim for entertaining clients; this isn't the case anymore, which is why it is essential to check with an accountant each year.

Things like heat, rent, light etc. only relate to your business. They can't be used for your home bills (they stay under drawings.) Also, those coffees I buy to write in a café? Sadly I can't claim for them even though I am working.

The next thing to look at is things like professional fees. You might belong to a professional guild or club. I am an RSA Fellow, and my yearly fee would split across each month on the cash flow forecasting sheet. You would do the same for any organisation you belong to.

Capital expenditure is for when you buy new pieces of equipment to run your business/career. It might be a new musical instrument, sewing machine, or computer, and this is one of those areas that the Government changes the payment policy regularly. Check with an accountant how you are allowed to spread the payments costs, and if you are allowed to claim for the whole amount of the item in one go, or spread it across five years, taking into account the decreasing value each year.

All of the above shouldn't be complicated. It is only inputting data that we know to be true and correct, and understanding the rules and ways that our government wants us to do that. There is nothing to be fearful of, if we can mark out time on our calendar each month to sit down and do it we won't end up at the end of the year in a big panic with piles of receipts in a shoe box. That was how I used to deal with my finances until I realised the fear and dread I was feeling wasn't actually about the figures, it was about the lack of understanding that I had around accounting and cash flow forecasting. Once I understood that it was only inputting data in the correct box, those feelings went away. Of course, there are still days when I doubt my abilities and wonder if I will ever be hired again (even the most successful people still feel this way.)

By gaining back control of your finances, rather than them controlling you, you will not only help your business, but it will also help to build your confidence and behave like a professional. When we begin to develop a professional structure and systems around us, others view us as professional and trust us with work, projects and sales. *Being professional is good for business.*

The next thing that I want to talk about is VAT. VAT stands for Value Added Tax. In the UK VAT is currently set at 20% but this can change. Other countries have different levels. For example, Turkey is set at 18%. As each country is different, I am only going to focus on the UK VAT law. Do you check with your own VAT office to find out what the rules are for your country?

In the UK you don't have to register for VAT unless your turnover reaches £85K (2018 figure). If you think that you are shortly going to approach that you need to inform the VAT office, and it is advisable to bring an accountant on board, as there is a certain way of filing VAT accounts.

The UK does allow you to register for VAT even if you aren't reaching the VAT threshold. There are pros and cons to this. Several photographers I know will register for VAT, as they continuously have to keep up-to-date with their expensive photographic equipment. If they register for VAT, they will be able to claim back all of the VAT they have made on purchases relating to their business. That could mean thousands of pounds reclaimed at the end of the year. So what are the cons? It means you have to file accounts more often across the year and you will become 20% more expensive to hire as a freelancer. It can make you appear more professional if you are selling business to business, as businesses can claim the VAT back as well. You need to decide what is right for you.

If you sell products, you need to check what the VAT rules are. By this I mean, check if by law you have to charge VAT on them. They might have specific VAT levels that aren't 20%. It sounds complicated, but again it is all about finding out what the rules are and then sticking to them. Technology and products are changing all the time, and the government tries to keep up with these changes. In 2016 they changed VAT rules for companies and individuals who sell digital products. If you write e-books, create online courses or offer paid for digital downloads you would have to register for VAT in the EU countries where the customer downloaded them, so if you are in the UK and someone in France wants to download your e-book, you would have to register for VAT in France. Obviously this is frustrating, and personally, I think it is ridiculous for a solo freelancer who is trying to make a living. The government has created something called VAT Moss Mini One Stop Shop Scheme that allows you to register and pay VAT due on sales of digital services to consumers in the EU. These laws change over time, so check with an accountant who is up-to-date with the VAT laws.

If you find that you do have to register for VAT you would add the percentage of VAT you have to pay (i.e. 20% in the UK) into the VAT column on your cash flow-forecasting sheet; this is money you have to collect and give to the government. Your sheet will now show you the amount of money you have left for your business each month and add up the difference in the net box. It will then show you if you are in profit or loss each month. Remember that being at a loss one-month isn't the end of the world. Money flows in and out of business all the time. We use credit cards to pay for items while we wait for invoices to clear, and when they clear, at the end of the month we can pay off our entire credit card bill. In the UK if you pay the balance of your credit card bill each month, it helps to raise your credit rating, which could be the difference between being accepted for a business loan, mortgage or investment or not.

All of these ways of managing your money can affect several areas of your life, both business and personal. Doesn't it feel like a good idea to take control of it yourself so that you can prepare for the future and reach your goals?

The other part of your finance toolbox is **bookkeeping**. When we are starting, we have to do many things on our own until we can earn enough to pay somebody to do it for us. Bookkeeping is one of those things. You might feel that not having two cups of coffee a day and having a bookkeeper instead is the best use of that money. Start with systems that are most beneficial to you. Each person will be different. What I want is for you to understand the basic systems so that when you hand the work over to someone else, you can not only explain what you want them to do but also be able to ask for information about your finances and understand the way it is presented to you.

Even in big businesses, it is useful for the CEO to have a look at the books, to check that there aren't mistakes, that there is enough money to cover plans they are making, and verifying that there isn't any theft or corruption happening within the company. You might be thinking 'I am never going to be a big business or a CEO." I want you to think like a CEO. Even if you are a solo freelancer, you represent your brand, company and reputation. Quite literally the buck stops with you. We can't blame others for not having a hold on our finances. It is our responsibility to check in and understand them from time to time as our career grows. Understanding the basics will help you to plan, build confidence and train others if you eventually take on employees of your own.

Basic bookkeeping doesn't have to be complicated. It is all about working out a system that works for you. Broken down it contains the following elements that we need to input each week or month:

1. Invoices you send out (your income)
2. Invoices/bills that you receive + pay.
3. Expenses relating to each job/project or your business overall.
4. Any VAT you have to pay if you're registered to pay VAT.
5. Any profit you have made.

As you did for the cash flow forecasting, bookkeeping is all about collecting those five pieces of data and ordering them by the job or by month. That information you add to the cash flow forecast sheet, and it is as simple as that.

I wasn't the best at school in math. Lessons in trigonometry and algebra went over my head. As a creative, I began to believe that I was no good at numbers and that accounts would be complicated and something I wouldn't be able to do. I want you to know the girl who scrapped through in math can now manage million-pound budgets, and I believe you can learn how to too.

Using the term 'no-good-at-numbers' is an excuse we tell ourselves, when in fact what we mean is *"I am frightened of numbers, and I don't understand what I need to do."* You could always find someone to help you and set a system up that works for you and isn't too much of a chore.

Do I love doing accounts? *Hell, no!* Do I find it boring inputting the data? *Yes, I do.* The difference I feel is that the fear has gone away. We will always have to do things that we don't love to make our business and career work. Accounts might be one of those things. It isn't as scary or as hard as you think. Follow the steps, ask for help and build it into your schedule. Managing your money is one of the most powerful gifts you can give yourself.

If you don't think that the creative industries can earn a decent living or contribute to the economy, think again. In the UK the creative industries exported £27billion of services in 2016. The creative industries account for 1 in 11 of all UK jobs. (2015 - www.thecreativeindustries.co.uk) Those aren't small figures. Being creative can be a sustainable, successful career. Managing how you earn income from it is the key.

6

Your Worth

Now that you have a handle on the figures and know where to find the help we can move on to understanding your worth.

Many of the women that I train on my courses or attend my lectures say that the thing they struggle the most with is their own worth. I regularly see them underselling themselves. Not only financially but also by devaluing the skills and experience they already have. In the UK girls outperform boys at school. That should mean we exceed them in the workplace and out-earn them as well. News reports in 2015-2016 were full of stories about women in corporate jobs in Hollywood standing up against the gender pay gap between men and women. I find it shocking that since 1916 when the suffragettes fought to give women the right to vote we are still having a debate about equal pay. If we outperform boys at school, why aren't we outperforming them in the workplace?

We still carry most of the childcare commitments during our life. We have to take breaks for maternity leave and pay for childcare if we want to return to work. Since having my son, I understand the difficulties of juggling work and family life. Having a family sadly can still affect our earning potential, but it isn't the only reason.

We know that we are equally as intelligent as men. At school we outperform them. We know that we are equally as creative as men and capable of having a freelance career or business regardless of whether we have children or not. So what is holding us back and why do we undervalue ourselves?

I was always shy at school. I told you about the stage fright I had to deal with and the tricks I learnt to make myself more confident. Your value is mainly rooted in confidence. Only when we feel confident about our abilities, knowledge or experience, do we value it. We always believe that we don't know enough, or we need to reach the top of something to prove our worth. I know how hard it is to work in male-dominated industries. I've worked in offices at newspapers and on film sets where 90% of the workforce were male.

Sometimes we need to stand up and draw attention to the work that we have done. You don't have to be aggressive or stand on top of the mountain, waiting to get attention. I will talk you through ways of gaining recognition of your work later on. Right now we need to deal with your worth.

The dictionary definition of worth is: "worth having/doing to be important or useful" " Enjoyable enough or producing enough advantages to make the necessary effort, risk, pain etc. seem acceptable."

Be worth it:

"to be of reasonable or good value for the price."

I want you to read that definition again for worth it:

"Enjoyable enough or producing enough advantages to make the necessary effort, risk, pain etc. seem acceptable."

Let's change - "seem acceptable" -with- "make-it-worth-having." I want you to start looking at all of the ways that clients, customers, friends, lovers and others believe that you're worth having in their lives, for us to do that I want you to look at the skills you already have. These are skills you already own. They might be a little rusty, and we can work with that.

We are going to start by looking at what I call the 'fun skills.' These are skills that you have and don't necessarily want to make a living from, but they are things you love doing and will find easy. They can be things like being able to horse ride, climb a mountain, know all the names of the plants in your garden or can draw a picture perfectly. They might be the ability to code software, and you have it as a hobby but don't want to own any money from it. You might make your clothes but don't want to be a fashion designer or else you are great at doing handstands and yoga. Write down every skill that you as a human being take pleasure in doing or else find it easy and effortless. These are personal skills; nothing related to your business. If you are struggling to fill the section in, ask your friends and family if there is something you do that they admire or think of you when they need help with something? Maybe you bake amazing brownies or can style an outfit like no one else.

Take a look at that list. How many things have you written down? Are there things on the list that you would love to learn more about or things that you would be happy to teach others to do? Put a cross next to the ones you want to know more about, and a tick next to the ones you would be happy to teach others. You may not have any ticks or X's, and that is fine. We have personal skills that we enjoy for ourselves, and they can stay that way.

In the same way that you made a list of your personal skills, now make a list of your 'career skills.' These are skills that you need for your career or future career plans. They could be a piece of software that you understand. They could be bookkeeping skills, confidence in public speaking. No matter how small you think, that skill is, write it down. You might be good at writing copy for websites, have an excellent manner on the telephone (this is a skill!), Or else you are brilliant at dancing. Again if you get stuck ask your friends and family what your business/career skills are. They might think of things that you overlooked as you find them effortless.

By the time you have finished, you should have a long list. Have a look at that list. Are there skills that can be grouped? I.e. computer skills, performance skills, writing skills etc. Are there any skills that you could teach and share with others? Are there ones that you would like to learn more about or improve? Put a tick next to all of the skills you are confident about. If you don't have any, try not to be so hard on yourself. There will be skills that you can do better than someone else. Have another look and get a friend to look at it for you. If we are going to make a successful creative career, we need to feel confident about some of the skills we have.

After doing this exercise, you should have a good idea of where your strengths lie. There might be some surprises on the list, things that you haven't thought of. What I want you to do now is to pull off five skills from either list that you feel confident about and could share with someone else. How could you share these skills? Could you run a workshop, write an article, create a blog post or make a how-to video series?

These five skills could help you in a number of ways. Firstly they prove that you are good at something already, without the need for further learning. Secondly, they are skills that you could share with others either for free or as a way to make some extra money while you build your career. And thirdly these are skills that I want you to fix the word 'expert' in front of. "I'm an expert in writing blog posts" or "I'm an expert in running art workshops".

How does using the term expert make you feel? Does it fill you with pride or do you feel like a fraud and that you need a PhD on something before you can be called an expert?

I want to share a secret with you. You only need to be one step ahead of someone for you to be an expert. The knowledge that you have right now will be worth something to someone. Somewhere in the world, someone will be looking for the information and skills that you hold.

A study by Heinz school saw male students put themselves forward again and again for opportunities over and above the female colleagues. They weren't always experts in what they said yes to, and others read a book on the subject before delivering a talk.

I'm not suggesting that you have to stand up in a theatre full of people to give a talk on one of those skills - but I would encourage you to believe that you can. If men can go off and read a book to allow themselves to be called an expert, we don't need to run off and become a PhD student to be an expert in something. If we all did that, then no information skills and experiences would be shared.

You are already an expert based on your own experiences and education. Many of the skills I have, I have taught myself. That doesn't make me less of an expert. In many ways, by learning skills through personal experience (like film production), I know more about it than someone at university learning through studying the theory. Having an educational stamp is a beautiful thing, but I don't want this to hold you back. There are a million things we could wish we had in place before I moved forward with our career. I used to say I needed new cameras, or another course before I was ready. In the end, all I needed to do was start and learn as I went along.

You have so much to offer, and so many skills you have learnt already by being on this planet. The key is to see them as valuable at work and worth something; not only to you but to others as well.

If you want to take this further, there are great sites out there that can help you find out what your top skill skills are. Through a series of questions, they help you to find out where your strengths lie.

I used the 'Gallup Strength Test.' They offer several packages, but I believe you only need to know what your top five strengths are. For a few dollars, they deliver them to you in great detail and tell you how you can use, develop and improve on those skills. I had a couple of surprises in mine that I didn't realise were my top skills, for the very reason that they were so instinctive to me, I overlooked them as a strength.

By understanding our skills and strengths, we can see the areas that we are good at and areas where we need some help. It is impossible for us to juggle everything long term. There will come a moment when we have to hire a bookkeeper or move out of the bedroom into a workshop. By valuing your strengths and skills, you can also look at ways of monetising some of them or sharing your knowledge to build your reputation and brand.

If you are struggling to believe in your worth, take another look at the goals you wanted to achieve. You wouldn't have written down something you didn't care about. You probably already understand most of the skills you need to have in place to achieve that goal, even if all of the skills are not your own. Some people find mood boards or vision boards helpful. In simple terms, this is a collage of images that represent something that you are aiming for. I have used it when saving for a holiday - sticking a picture of the bright white beach somewhere, where I will see it each day. By keeping it in my mind, it encouraged me to save my money and get my holiday booked when I wanted it. If visuals aren't your thing, you might prefer quotes to help you build your confidence and belief in yourself. I love quotes as they distil a small piece of wisdom quickly and with impact.

If you are still unsure about your worthiness, make a list of all the things that you have achieved. Start by focusing only on this week. Did you manage to build a new contact, or take a walk at lunchtime to improve your health? Then move onto the bigger picture. What things have you achieved in your life that you are proud of? They don't have to be a huge life-changing event. They have to be personal to you and something that makes you smile when you think about it. Write these down so you can read them on 'bad days'.

The final thing I want you to do involves finding out what others think is your worth. Excluding your parents, ask twenty friends or family what they value about you. It can be related to skills, strengths or something personal. Write all of their answers down. These 'value truths' will help you through the days when self-doubt and fear take over. We all have days like this. That is a normal part of growing and pushing ourselves forward. If we felt comfortable all of the time, we wouldn't be developing ourselves, and our careers. Knowing how to cope with those 'dark days' is the most powerful tool we can find.

7

Pricing your goods and services.

There is a certain amount of alchemy involved in pricing your goods and services. There are fixed elements which you can't change without consequences and others that require reputation, trust, and a bit of confidence.

Creatives often find it hard to price their goods or services correctly. They enjoy the process of creating so much that they can work on something for hours and then struggle to recoup the costs of all of that work.

When we price goods or services, we are (at a basic level) exchanging the time it took us to do something, with the monetary value of that time. How we work out that monetary value is a series of questions you need to ask yourself. I will come to these in a moment.

If we are selling a product, we know how long it took us to create it. We know how much it costs in the primary materials (if it is a physical product. I will talk about digital projects separately.) Also, we know how much the packaging and marketing costs to put that product out into the world. All of these factors we call a BASE COST.

To find out how to price your goods and services here are a few questions to help you.

1. How much per hour or day do you want to be paid for your time?
2. How much does it cost to prototype your product?
3. If you are providing a service, how, much pre and post prep does it take to deliver the service?
4. How much travel have you had to do to create your product or service? You will need to work out the mileage and time.
5. How much do you spend on studio, office, rent, heat, phone calls etc.?
6. How much does your website cost to host, design and update?
7. What are your postal costs for one product including the packaging?
8. What other costs do you have to cover to create your product or deliver your service? These can be things like insurance, Guild membership, marketing, advertising etc.?

This list of questions will change depending on your product or service. (Even if you deliver a digital service or products you will have Base Costs). There are fixed elements of your Base Costs, like your time, materials, business, insurance, studio costs etc. The only way you can change these is to use different materials, move studios or work out a way of making the product in less time. A warning though! If you change your materials, packaging etc., you might be changing your customer profiling. If we make something more expensive or with cheaper materials, we will be speaking and selling to a different set of customers, which doesn't mean it might not be a good solution for you. What it does mean is that there are consequences for each change or decision that you make, and you need to be aware of them.

Work through that list of Base Cost questions and add anything else that you need to create your product or service. Now you have those elements written down, take a look at them. Are there any surprises? Is there anything you have forgotten? Is this something that you need but can't afford the moment? In the beginning, we might be doing our own package design and marketing. As you grow, you can outsource this, so that you can focus on your creative work and not juggle several things at once.

Add to the list anything that you would love to do/have to bring that product or service to market. It might be hiring a member of staff to assist you or a PR company. I want you to add these elements to the list so that you can prepare for those future costs. They may not be part of your expenses right now, but if they can help you deliver the best product or service in the future, it is essential to know what they are now, and how much they will cost to have.

Remember those five-year goals? Adding in those 'Wish List' future elements to our planning helps us to prepare financially for the future. It also tells us how long it would take to add those elements and whether our products and services are correctly priced for when we want to bring those future elements into action.

Go back to that list you have made of the base costs and fill in the facts. How many hours does it take you to make the product or service, how much does prototyping and testing cost, how much will it cost to hire an assistant or buy a piece of manufacturing equipment? Note all of these figures down. If you don't know them at the moment, leave a space and come back to it. Add all of the totals that you have and this will give you your BASE COST.

Does this price surprise you? Is it more or less than you expected? Have you correctly priced each hour it takes to do your job? In the UK the minimum wage for over 21-year-olds is £7.38. If you are well trained, have a degree or industry experience, are an expert in what you do (remember if you own those skills, you are an expert) you should be charging a decent hourly rate. I would expect you to be asking for over £15 per hour. Look at industries like plumbing and electrics. They charge over £20 per hour. They are skilled individuals offering a service. Your business/career might be as a creative, but you are still delivering a specialised service. Once we value our worth, we will become more confident about charging a decent price per hour.

The next parts of pricing that we have to think about are the prices you want to charge for your product or service and how much profit you will make.

Pricing your product or service I believe is closely related to your work. When I started, I was terrible at pricing my photography work. Clients would haggle over the price, or I would underestimate the amount of time I need to drive to the location, do the shoot and all of the post-production before I delivered the finished work to the client. It took a few trials and errors, (and being strong enough to say no to clients that haggled over the price) for me to work out what to charge and stick to it. Sure, I lost some potential clients/customers in the process, but these weren't my correct clients and customers. By customer profiling the market I wanted to enter into, I was able to find out who my direct competitors were, and examine their pricing and marketing.

When you are trying to price your goods and services, it is a valuable part of the process to look at your competitors. They might be competitors in the same location as you, or working internationally. Look at their pricing. Do they have clear pricing for the goods or services that they offer? Do they offer discounts for specific packages or hold sales? When we look at our competitor's pricing, we call it benchmarking. Benchmarking is the next element of pricing.

I want you to look at three of your competitors' pricing. You can look at their websites or ask someone who has hired them. If they are in another town and not a direct threat, you can telephone or email them to ask for their advice; this is an excellent habit to start. All they can do is say no, but they might say yes as well. Examine their pricing structure. Are they clear about how much the product or service costs? Do they have added extras that they offer or are they charging per hour or for the cost of the job? Write all of these details down.

Next look at three competitors that you aspire to become in the future. These can be individuals or businesses. They must be working in your industry and more prominent than you are at the moment. They may not show their pricing, or it might be hard to find out, but not impossible. Find out what pricing structure they use, how much their product or service costs and how they sell their product or service. By that I mean, what language do they use to market themselves, their product or service. Do they use images or ideas? Is it all based on testimonials?

Write down their prices and describe what they are offering for that price. Next, I want you to explain how they sell themselves in one paragraph. Have a look at what they do that is different from your own career/business. Write down five things that you would like to be able to do for your business/career in the future that they are offering their clients and customers. These five things should make up your aspirational goals, and you need to add them to the description of your goals for the future. Having something to aim for helps us to focus, and it also makes it easier to communicate what our goals are. If we have no idea what we are aiming for, we can end up running around in circles and not getting anywhere.

Although your price will have base costs added, there is an element of aspirational value that you may consider adding in the future. Aspirational value isn't something you can add at the beginning of your career. It takes time to build a reputation, brand and trust. All of these elements make up aspirational pricing. If you are a fashion designer straight out of college, you need to build a fan base before you can start charging couture prices. It is the same if you're offering a service; you need to create trust with new clients before you can charge aspirational prices.

The prices that I charge for my work are 95% more than the rates I charged to my work eight years ago. It has taken that amount of time for me to develop my work, build a reputation, and gain experience and knowledge. All of which adds value to what I now deliver. If I had tried to charge these prices at the beginning, no-one would have hired me. I didn't have enough previous experience or trusted client experiences that I could share. Aspirational value isn't an impossible thing to aim for, but it does take time, and nerves of steel! Aspirational value also links to believing your worth and having the confidence to ask for it. I will cover more about this in the negotiation section.

So how do you price your goods and services to make sure you have a profit? Before I talk about pricing services for profit, I want to talk about how you would find the wholesale price of your products. When we make something, we don't necessarily want to have to be the main supplier or seller of that product. (Remember that I said we want to make sure in the future we are not doing everything, only focusing on doing our creative work?) There may come the point where you want to get your product out to a new market or into an upmarket boutique, and you need to work out what the wholesale price of your product would be. All of the elements that make up the price remain the same (you need to cover your costs), and your profit will now come from the difference between the cost and the wholesale price.

Let's talk about what goes into your wholesale price and why it differs store to store. You need to make a profit, and the store does too. The store has overheads just as you do. They need to pay staff wages, lighting, business rates, advertising etc. The store's position will depend on how high the wholesale price is. Selling your products to a supermarket will not generate the same amount as selling at the top luxury store in central London. Not only are their costs different, but their customers are as well.

Tip: Even though you are selling business to business before you approach any store make sure you do your homework and find out if their customers are right for your products, brand etc.

BASE COST: Finding the→ Wholesale Price

Low-end	Mid range	High-end store
Multiply the base cost by 2.4	Multiply the base cost by 2.5	Multiply the base cost by 2.7

Using the above formula, let's imagine that our base cost is £1 or $1, and we'll work through each store wholesale price.

Low end (supermarket)
= Base cost = £1/$1 x 2.4 = £2.40 or $2.40

Mid range
= Base cost = £1/$1 x 2.5 = £2.50 or $2.50

High end
= Base cost = £1/$1 x 2.7 = £2.70 or $2.70

Next, the wholesaler needs to add more to that price to make sure they earn a profit; this would be called the Registered Retail Price or RRP. As with the wholesale price, the amount you multiply the wholesale price by will depend on the store.

Wholesale

Price multiply   Low end------→2.8

Mid range----→3.2

High end -----→3.7

Using the formula above let's work through the figures again.

Low end

Wholesale price = £2.40/ $2.40 x 2.8 = £6.72/ $6.72

Mid range

Wholesale price = £2.50/ $2.50 x 3.2 = £8.00/ $8.00

High end

Wholesale price = £2.70/ $2.70 x 3.7 = £9.99/ $9.99

When I first worked through these figures, I was shocked at the difference between the base cost and the RRP. If your product has cost you £1/$1 to create and it now costs £$9.99 to sell, what questions does that raise?

- Is that too expensive?
- Can I sell enough?
- What sort of customers are we now talking to?

If your product costs £10 or £100 to create it will now cost £99.90 or £999 as a retail price. £100-£999 is a considerable jump. You might be a jewellery designer with high base costs. Suddenly you have to think about whether you can change your manufacturing to reduce the base cost, or else discover that the clientele who can afford the retail price is from a completely different demographic, which has consequences on all of your marketing, packaging etc.

You should do this exercise for all of your work if you make products, even if you aren't selling to wholesale. It will let you see how much your retail price should be. Although you're not selling to wholesale now, you may want to in the future. What you don't want to do is suddenly find that you have to raise your prices or that you are making a loss to sell to wholesale. Too often on Internet sites like FOLKSY and ETSY, I see this mistake repeated again and again. The prices only cover their costs, and if they ever wanted to sell wholesale, their profit margin would be nil or in deficit.

Starting as if you are already successful, will not only make others treat you professionally, it will also protect you for the future when you want to expand and grow. I don't want you to find yourself in an awkward position of having to dramatically raise your prices or discover that your client base has to change completely.

Base costs are hard to change. Every change you make (whether manufacturing costs or using different materials) will have a dramatic effect on your business. You may have to manufacture many and remove the handmade element of your work to make a profit. Alternatively, you have to charge more, which changes who your customers and clients are. Luxury brands take time to build, and you need to understand the trends and requirements to make that successful. Nothing is impossible though. You need to decide what is right for you and your work, and how you go about achieving it.

If like me, your business offers services, you will still have to think about pricing. You will have a base cost which is the time it takes you to create that service for the first time, the cost of your office, heat, lighting etc. and any travel costs, if you deliver that service in person.

Obviously, travel costs will change from job to job, and once you have created the service once, you shouldn't have to spend the same amount of preparation time on it when you deliver it a second time. What I don't want you to do is to reduce that base cost when you deliver it a second time. It may have taken you three days to create it once, so it is essential to make sure you ask for that each time.

Services are difficult to price correctly, as there is a certain amount of uncertainty that goes into building them. They often don't have the physical item to show for the work you have created, but they are still valuable. These are the cost factors that I want you to think about if you are offering a service:

- The time it takes to create it once.
- Any materials you need to use
- Overhead Costs
  -stationary/printing/postage/telephone
  -office/studio costs
  - heating/electric/gas at office/studio
- Travel costs (change with each job)
- Staff costs to create or deliver it.
- Marketing/Publicity
- Professional insurance covering public liability.
- Follow up services/feedback/collecting testimonies (include this time.)
- If you are a photographer – remember to include the processing costs. How long does it take you to process and deliver the work?

This list is not exhaustive - you will have preparation costs only you are aware of. It is essential to include them as you should charge the same price each time you deliver. You may need to update your service from time to time, and those preparation costs will allow you to do it.

You won't have a wholesale or RRP (registered retail price), but you will have an idea of how much profit you would like to make.

When I was starting, it felt impossible for me to charge for all of the hours that I put into creating my lessons, courses and coaching packages. I was worried that I didn't have enough experience under my belt; I couldn't charge what I needed to cover my costs. So to still be able to offer my services to clients and customers I negotiated on extras-like petrol costs, subsistence (meals). As I became more confident and built on my reputation and experience, I was able to add what I call 'aspirational cost.'

Aspirational costs are related to your education, skills, knowledge, profile, experience and reputation. They will differ from person to person and country to country. Aspirational costs take time to build, often years. They also take confidence and research to ask for them. Remember I told you the story that when I was starting my fees were low and now they are 95% higher. I offer a similar service to when I started, but my knowledge base and reputation has grown so that 95% pays for that reputation and they want me to deliver the service rather than someone else, as my proven track record produces results which equate to value for money. As I mentioned before, there is an element of alchemy to this process. We will look at it in more depth later on.

The one thing I want you to keep in your mind during all of this pricing process is your customer. Even if you are selling business to business you know from doing the customer profiling exercise that you still have a customer at the company you are communicating with, plus an ideal customer that you want.

If you can't charge what you need to cover your costs for delivering your service, is there a way to create different packages? Gold, silver and bronze packages allow you to provide your service to those that want it, but can't afford it. Gold packages, which include added extras or more of your time, you would charge a premium for them. Silver would also offer some extras but less of your time, and bronze would be a basic service with no extras. The sales you make from the gold and silver packages would allow you to offer the services to those less able to afford it on the bronze package.

The other way to deliver your service at the price you need is to not sell it directly to individual customers. Instead, you would approach institutions like schools, councils, arts organisations etc., who would buy your service for a price relating to the number of people who would take it. The institution would find the consumers, which would reduce your marketing costs and time; this would allow you to charge slightly less as a 'buy-out-price.' Alternatively, if you can add aspirational costs, you can sell the package at a high price to an institution; backed up with research and case studies about the benefits the service will bring to their clients. I always offer a long-term element to these packages such as updates, mentoring or networking opportunities for the consumers - so that the institution has something extra to provide their clients that they wouldn't be able to get if they bought the course as an individual.

What you charge is up to you. What you need to make sure is that you think about your customer, costs and profits, so that you can deliver the product and service, not once, but several times and make a healthy profit.

We can use A and B testing if we are unsure of what to charge. I love this example of A and B testing for two shirts. They were both manufactured for precisely the same cost, but one came with a collar.

The company decided that, as they weren't selling many of the shirts with the collar, they would raise the price of it. It might feel like a counterintuitive thing to do, but at the end of the testing period, they had sold many more of garment B. Psychologically by seeing garment B at a higher price the customer valued it more and chose it over garment A.

You might find that by charging more for your product and service your customers/clients value it more and make a purchase.

Have a look at your favourite shops over the next week. Take a look at the items you like and their prices. You can take the RRP and work backwards to find an approximate base cost price. It might surprise you. When a T-shirt costs £2 at base cost, you begin to wonder how much wage the person earned who sewed it together. Every pricing decision we make has a consequence.

8

Dealing With Fear
And Procrastination

At some point in our day, week, month or life - procrastination can hit us. The feelings of enthusiasm fade away, replaced by a dread of the task ahead. Or else we become sullen teenagers shouting that the world is so unfair. Sound familiar? I have days like this. I know what I need to do to move my business forward, but instead, that pile of washing up suddenly feels like the most important thing to deal with in the world. You might be one of those lucky people who never procrastinated about anything. If you are, I admire you greatly and am equally exhausted wondering how you fit it all in! It is still beneficial for you to understand where procrastination comes from in case you have a friend or colleague suffering from it.

For the rest of us, I want us to go back to the very beginning of when we first began to procrastinate. Were you a great student at school who finished their homework in plenty of time, planned every family holiday, and knew what your hours and minutes were going to be filled with one day to the next?

Or were you a student who left their homework until the last minute, sitting up all night writing an essay? Did you prefer to make no plans at all and dive into situations and plan as you went along?

Or did you wake up most days not wanting to do anything? You were sleepwalking through classes, as they didn't interest you at all? You had no hobbies or passions and fumbled along until you found something you loved or were good at?

There is no right or wrong way to choose to live your life. I am usually a mixture of the three examples above. Some of my days have sharp focus, others I prefer spontaneous events filling up the day, and on days I feel frustrated or have little or no interest in doing anything; the day fades into the night without me even noticing.

We are all granted 24 hours a day. What we do with those hours is mostly up to us. Of course, life, children, and responsibilities make themselves known and demand some of those 24 hours; the rest we need to make the best use of that we can.

We started at the beginning of our life and our connection to procrastination, I want us to now begin at the end.

When I was four years old, my father left for good. It was in the 1970s when divorce wasn't as common as it is now. My mother was left with a babe in arms and me a headstrong four-year-old. I can only imagine that it was one of the most difficult and lonely times in her life. I never got to ask her though, as she died of breast cancer when I was nine, and my baby brother was seven. You might be wondering why I am telling you this story. I wanted to show you that life handed me a hand that told me life is short and incredibly precious. I want you to remember this too.

I'm now older than my mother ever was which gives me a sense of responsibility for the years ahead. Those are years she didn't get to live. Even though I learnt how short life is at a young age, I still have days when I procrastinate. But having an understanding of the end of your life will help you plan out the beginning. I don't want us to get morbid about this; I want us to be excited that we can (to a degree) take control of our lives and choices and make a 'life plan' starting with the end.

I want you to step into my mother's shoes for a moment. She knew the end was coming, what would you want the world to say about you when you are gone? What would you like to be remembered as? What achievements did you make in your life? Who else did you help along the way? What did you give back to the world? What would people say about you when you are gone?

My mother had a send-off overflowing with people gathered from all over the world. People sent poems and heartfelt letters from the four corners of the globe. I know this as I have kept them. She touched people, helped those less fortunate and cared for everyone she came into contact with. She had set up her own business before she died and I'm sure if she had lived it would have been a great success.

How would you like to be remembered? Are you doing what you have started now, or has it turned into something different? Have you done charity work? Are you training for the next generation coming up the ranks? Are you giving part of your profits away or doing volunteer work? Have you built a successful business that you sold off years before your retirement?

Put as much detail down as possible. It can help to write in the third person to give yourself some distance and allow you to write freely. Have a look at everything you have written. Does this sound like the person you are now or the person you wish to become? What changes or plans do you need to make for this to happen? Do you need to change the structure of your business/career to make these plans work? Do you need to charge more for your products or services to be able to give something back?

By thinking about the end, we can plan for the beginning.

Tip: This is a useful way to plan all projects, no matter how big or small. Look at the end and what you want the project to achieve, then work backwards looking at all of the elements you need to complete for it to be a success.

Now that we have a vision of what we want to become, and achieve, we can have a real look at procrastination.

As Charles Dickens said

"Procrastination is the thief of time, collar him."

We may not be able to 'cure' procrastination completely, but we can work out when it strikes and why which will help us to make a plan to deal with it at those times.

Procrastination doesn't always appear because we are feeling lazy. Sometimes there are deep-rooted reasons why we procrastinate.

Think about the times that you were procrastinating.

- What were you attempting to do when procrastination struck?
- How were you feeling at the time?
- How did the procrastination make you feel (be honest with yourself)?
- Did you complete the task?
- If yes, how did you manage to stop procrastinating and complete the task?
- If not, what stopped you/thoughts/feelings.
- How did you feel when you did complete the task?

Have a close look at your answers. Does a pattern appear? Do you have the same thoughts and feelings every time you procrastinate?

Procrastination is often linked to fear. We are fearful of making a mistake, or because we don't know enough about the subject, so we end up not finishing the project. We can also be fearful of success.

We worry that we will have more to do, have to prove ourselves to a broader audience or hire staff if we are successful. Procrastination can also be linked to imposter syndrome. We don't believe in our abilities and worry that someone will 'find us out,' tap us on the shoulder and ask us to leave. All of these thoughts are perfectly natural, and you are not alone in feeling them. I have these types of thoughts every time I start a new project or take on a new client. We can have those feelings; it is what we do with them that is the important thing. (I'll talk more about imposter syndrome in a moment).

Life is full of struggles. It is all about working out which ones you want to spend your time battling. We want to make sure that procrastination isn't one of them.

Look back at your notes; do you recognise moments when you are fearful? Is it because of success, our abilities or something else?

Write down what drives your procrastination. Can you think of ways you can combat it? Write down who can help you, or systems you can put in place to make it easier to manage.

Studies have shown that runners are more successful with a running buddy; maybe you would find it useful to have an accountability partner to help you through the procrastination. Sometimes we struggle to get everything done on our own. Having an accountability partner can help you to succeed and get a project finished. They are especially helpful if you are someone who suffers from procrastination or Imposter Syndrome. I've used them myself, and they can be a great support.

If your procrastination comes from fear, what is it a fear of?

- Fear of failure
- Fear of the unknown
- Fear of lack of knowledge
- Fear of being found out – Imposter Syndrome

- Fear of making a fool of yourself
- Fear of Success
- Fear of not being perfect
- Fear of not finishing
- Fear of starting....

Only when we identify where the fear is coming from can we work out a strategy to deal with it.

On any day I can feel many fears around the work I am doing. I worry that no one will care about the work, or that I won't have time to finish it, and on really bad days I have Imposter Syndrome.

Imposter Syndrome can hit you at any stage in your career. It doesn't care if you are starting or have been on this path for decades. At some point, you will be called upon to step out of your comfort zone and deliver. It might be a speech to a room full of school children, or a TED talk to an audience of millions, you would still end up feeling the same way- feeling like you don't know enough, and that someone in the room will call you on it.

You're not alone with these feelings. 78% of people will experience Imposter Syndrome during their career. Often it is the people at the height of their career who suffer with it the most.

This is a list of well-known professionals who have talked about their own experience of Imposter Syndrome.

- Kate Winslet
- Emma Watson
- Lupita Nyong'o
- Ryan Reynolds
- Meryl Streep
- Tina Fey
- Tom Hanks

- Sheryl Sandberg
- Serena Williams
- Maya Angelou
- Arianna Huffington
- Lady Gaga
- Neil Gaiman

It's quite an impressive list. I include it to let you know that you aren't alone. It often strikes when we are moving to the next level of our career.

Life gives us opportunities every day; it is our job to spot them when they come along, grab them with both hands and act on them; otherwise, they fade away. The truth is we will never be prepared enough; we'll never know everything, or be the most qualified person in the world.

When I was six years old, I had a terrible case of chicken pox. I stayed home for what felt like months. Books, stickers and my doll's house were all I had for company. (These were the days before kids had TVs and electronic gadgets in every room.) The days dragged but what I remember most about this time was having time to think. I don't mean thinking about the weather, or what I was missing out on at school; this was the first time I remember having huge thoughts about the world. I thought about the life I had in front of me and all of the books I wanted to read. I thought about Peter Pan – The boy who never grew up. I suddenly realised that I wouldn't be a kid forever, that I would never have time to read all the books I wanted to, and I would never know all of the knowledge in the world. Big thoughts for a little kid aged 6!

It was at that moment I realised grown-ups don't know everything either. When you are feeling scared and imposter syndrome strikes, it is worth remembering that the adults in the room don't know everything. They are making things up and learning as they go on. No one knows everything. All you have to be is one step ahead of all the people you are talking to, or else sharing an experience, or skill they know nothing about.

Women are taught at schools to do good work, research, work hard and behave. We are led to believe that our work must be perfect before we can show it to the world. I have some news for you – perfect doesn't exist. No matter how much we fiddle or try to improve our work, it will never be perfect. Perfect can't exist because the world isn't perfect. We can do our best, prepare and feel confident about what we are putting out into the world, but at some moment you will have to send it out before it is 100% ready. You will need to show it to the world and get feedback and opinions that aren't your own. Only when we share something can we improve on it.

The Japanese have a beautiful way of working with art objects. They believe that art cannot be perfect to be beautiful. They call it Wabi-Sabi – it is a way of looking at the world through the acceptance of transience and imperfection. I like this idea, as it is often the flaw that gives an object, or person its character. Most of the mugs in my home are handmade. I love the tactile, wonky quality of them all. I have favourite ones for certain drinks – coffee in a heavy bottomed one, and herbal teas in a fine one with a handle that seems to hug my hand. None of these objects I would call perfect- I would call them beautiful though.

Think of your work in the same way. Can you start before you are ready, or put your project out into the world before you are 100% sure it is perfect? If we always wait for things to be perfect, we never achieve anything. We can be as ready as we can be, but sometimes we need to share our work for it to grow beyond ourselves.

Fear of success is a tough one to deal with. It isn't rooted in anything tangible, only in our predictions of what might happen. We worry that we won't be ready, that it will generate more work than we can deal with, or that we'll get found out. (Good old imposter syndrome raising his head again!) All of these fears are valid, but they can't be proven to happen yet. We can predict that they may arise based on previous knowledge, other's experiences and research. If this is the case, you can have a plan B action ready for when you get more orders, or your course is such a success that you need to hire an assistant, or virtual PA to manage all of the emails. Having this plan B in the wings will allow the fear of success to subside while you get on with the business of creating.

Fear of success can be linked to the fear of your career/business growing more than you are comfortable with. Maybe friends and family have encouraged you to grow when you would be more comfortable staying small. Only you can decide how big you want your business or career to be. There are many small businesses, and comfortable freelancers, working out in the world without feeling the need to turn their work into a fortune 500 company. Go back to your goal setting and work out what will make you happy and comfortable with enough income to keep the lifestyle you want. Once you know those facts, you know what to aim for. You are the person choosing which path you take, or which opportunities you grab or not. We are the makers of our destinies. Deciding how we plan for that is the only way we find out which path to choose.

There will always be days we feel fearful. Even people working for others 9-5 each day, will have moments of panic and doubt. All humans think this way. And if they don't, they are either lying or edging towards the psychopath spectrum! You need to find tools and people who can help you through those fearful times so that you can move forward and share your creative talent with the world.

Remember that no adult knows everything; we have a right to take the platform as well and share the skills and experiences we have. There might be others in our field doing similar things to you, remember that you are unique and no one will be doing them the way you do.

One of the best things I learnt to help me get over the fear of starting was to stop comparing my beginning to someone's middle. It doesn't matter if you start your career when you are 22 or 55; the important thing is that you start (with the right tools and support of course!)

9

Change And Uncertainty – Making The Money Go A Long Way.

This is the moment when I ask you to have an honest chat with yourself. The freelance life isn't for everyone. There will be lean times and moments when you wonder if you will ever work again. With that comes moments of delight when you know you can book three months off for the winter, or take the day off and drive to the beach as the sun is shining.

When I started my career as a photojournalist in London, I worked nights as a waitress to cover my bills while I built my reputation. It was a sweet day when I was able to hand in my notice and hang up my apron for the last time. I learnt a lot about how to deal with difficult customers (drunken stockbrokers were regulars), how to smile and make someone's experience special, how to sell add-ons and bonuses (upselling – do you want a side salad with that), and how to work really long hours without falling asleep on the job. (The last skill I think had more to do with being young and energetic!) It certainly taught me that if I really wanted something, I would do everything I could to make it work.

When we are building our career, there may be moments when we have to take on work to pay the bills. We need to make sure that this is for the short term, and that your career doesn't fill up with projects you aren't passionate about. So how can we do that without losing our focus?

Back at the beginning, I asked you to look at your skill set and circle five skills that you felt confident about and could share with others. Have another look at those skills. We'll come back to them in a moment.

In my career, I have been freelance for over 24 years. One of the greatest tools I discovered was to plan for the lean times, even if they never came. When we get paid for a job, it is important to remember that 20% of that cash isn't ours. That 20% goes off to pay taxes. I realised that if I automatically deducted 20% each time I was paid, and put it into a saving account, I would have my entire tax ready by the end of the year. More importantly, I saved 20% even if I hadn't reached the tax income threshold. Adding to this 20% allowed me to save two months of living costs over the course of a year, without much effort.

By putting a couple of month's worth of living costs into a savings account, it meant three things when I was starting.

1. There were some emergency funds if a client didn't pay me on time.
2. At the end of the year, I could use some of the money (if I didn't need it) to upgrade my equipment or pay for a course to improve my skills.
3. It could act as a nest egg, so that if I wanted to take time off to complete a passion project – I knew that I had a couple of months covered.

(A Passion Project: This is a project that you complete for yourself rather than a client. It turns into a body of work that showcases your skills, and could be used in the future to attract new clients or audiences).

Having a nest egg helps you during lean times, during illness or when something goes wrong. Never feel resentment about paying taxes. I always feel happy about handing over some tax at the end of the year, as it proves I earned enough to pay tax. I'm putting money back into society, and it covers things like my healthcare. (In the UK our taxes pay for our National Health Service – we are fortunate to have it.)

Now we have planned to make a nest egg; we need to plan how to make an income when we are looking for new clients and customers. Take another look at those five skills that you said you would be confident sharing with someone else. Could you create a help-sheet of how to do it, or record a short 'how-to' video? Alternatively, could you create a simple e-book about the topic? You might be thinking "But I don't know how to do that." Let me assure you that there are lots of simple ways to create these without spending any money. The world of skill sharing and online education has exploded over the last few years. By sharing your skills and knowledge this way, you can supplement your income. I'm not talking about thousands of pounds/dollars coming your way (although there are examples of people earning those types of figures.) I'm talking about making a few £100/$100 while you sleep. By sharing your knowledge this way, you not only feel a sense of achievement, but you also pass your expertise onto a wider audience. You can become a trusted leader/expert in your field, you attract new clients and customers, plus you make some passive income from doing one piece of work.

You might be a dance teacher who works with special needs students or has started your own dance company. Somewhere, someone will want to know how to do that. It can be a simple video series explaining how they can set up their own company that they pay to download. Or you can create a teaching pack that you get printed and post out to them when they purchase it through your website. Alternatively, you could build a whole online course and sell it to the next generation of dancers?

This formula can work with any industry. Ask what people need help with and think about who would be interested in the knowledge you have to share. You only need to create this piece of work once for it to continue to generate income.

The magic formula is to create at least three income streams.

1. One while you sleep; a product that you can make once and sell again, and again.
2. The second is one that comes from working directly with clients and customers.
3. The third income stream comes from looking at what you already have, and using it to create something you can sell again, and again.

Is there something you can create that you can sell again and again? It could be a print of your artwork, a dance course, a ready-to-wear dress or a lecture series. Whatever it is, it needs to be popular, and something you can sell again and again with little effort. By little effort, I mean not having to go back to the drawing board each time and invent something new.

For artists, it might be holding an 'under the bed sale' – pulling out artwork that hasn't sold, and getting a group of you together to have a flash sale. (The run-up to holiday seasons work well for this type of show).

If you are a dancer, you might organise a taster session price for someone who isn't sure about taking your class. They could pay for a taster session, and then they get that price refunded when they book a block of classes.

Having something you have already created makes it much easier to deliver at short notice, or when you see a gap in your client's work. It is also a way to test your product and services on a new group of people.

You can include your previous clients and customers in these events. It is seven times harder to find new clients than it is to keep the one you have, which is why it is so important to make them feel special. You want them to come back and buy from you again and again. You can send them offers, or give them a small gift with every purchase they make. Vouchers or loyalty cards work well for products and services.

Think of five ways that you could make your customer or clients feel special and buy from or hire you again. If you are stuck coming up with ideas, think about being a customer. Where do you buy from again and again? What makes you go back to that store or online shop? It might be their excellent customer service, free postage, or that they send you interesting content or vouchers. If it is a service that you use, why do you keep using it? Are they reliable, make you feel good or offer you discounts and upgrades? What sort of things could you provide to make people return again and again?

Lastly, I want to talk more about your passion projects. When we are creating our work to make an income out of it, we can get lost in the mundane of everyday life. We forget what our passion was when we started our career. I don't want this to happen to you. One of the ways I found to avoid this was to create projects only for me between the paid work.

My passion projects might have had a life in the world after I completed them; the difference was that I didn't begin them thinking that they would have to earn money. Passion projects should be just that – all about passion. You might want to try something new that excites you, but you're not sure if it will sell. I say go for it to bring some passion back into your career. (That's what the nest egg is partly there to help us do.)

I believe that all photographers should have passion projects, having worked as one myself. It is often the only way to be able to complete a large body of work. You may publish it afterwards, or a few items may find their way into your portfolio. What it allows you to do is to develop your narrative skills and show off your best work, without worrying if it is right for the client. These passion projects can apply to sculptures, artists, dancers and designers as well.

Is there something you would love to do but believe that money or clients are holding you back?

In as much detail as possible think about what your dream passion project would be. If money or time were no object, what would you love to create? How long would it take you to complete it? Days, weeks or years? When would you like to start it? What one thing is holding you back (be honest with yourself?) How would you move that obstacle? If it is money, could you Crowdfund it? If it is time, how could you carve out an hour a day or week for your project?

Passion projects can also be useful ways of attracting new clients and customers. (Don't think this way when you start. It should be about passion, not the paycheck!)

I often tell my students that if they want to film a campaign for Nike, then they should shoot a campaign for Nike! If Nike hasn't called and hired them, then there is nothing stopping them from creating their own Nike campaign and sharing it online or with an advertising agency they would like to work for.

Sometimes you need to prove to a dream client that you can do it before they give you the dream job. It might feel like a counterintuitive thing to do it this way round, but in the world of digital sharing, it can often be the best way to get your work seen by that dream client.

Your own projects are never a waste of time. They allow you to experiment without the constraints of a client brief or budget. They let you try out new ways of doing things or show off your best work. They may end up getting you new jobs or showcasing a new idea on your website. And they can ignite your passion again. You can never underestimate how important that is.

Build them into your year's schedule, so that you have something to do during the quiet times as well. When I worked in the film industry my quiet times were during the winter months. Rather than worrying about these quiet times, I looked forward to them. With my nest egg saved I was able to complete a passion project, take a retreat, or else fly somewhere warm and work from my laptop on a beach.

Being freelance has to come with benefits to outweigh the risks. It is your chance to build the kind of working life you want to achieve. Making sure you plan for the lean times is the strongest way for you to be able to succeed.

10

Negotiation

I f I was to ask you how many times you had negotiated a raise or for a higher fee I would take a rough guess, and say that you could count the times on one hand or not at all. The word negotiation made me think of hard-hitting boardrooms or peace negotiations in war zones. What it didn't conjure up for me was a strong, calm woman, negotiating a raise. I began to wonder why. A quick survey of my female friends confirmed what I thought to be true; women tend not to negotiate. Straight out of college or university men are more inclined to negotiate their first job, and this immediately gives them an advantage as they can build on this increase in wages year on year. When researchers asked men and women to pay what they thought their work was worth, men paid themselves 68% more. Shocked? I was. When those same women looked at a sheet of what others had paid themselves, they chose the average price. This told me that women negotiate better when they can research the facts first. So how does all of this relate to the creative industries? At some point in our careers, we will all have to negotiate, whether that is for a higher fee, rights and responsibilities, holiday pay or extra benefits. Even if you are a solo artist, you will come into contact with galleries, agents, customers etc. at some point in your life and the way that you deal with all of these individuals will be through negotiation.

I believe negotiation skills are one of the most powerful things you can teach a woman to do. Regularly I am told that negotiation is hard, uncomfortable, embarrassing, money grabbing, aggressive, scary etc. We might feel all or one of these things at some point when we are negotiating, and I want to tell you that you can overcome all of them.

Let's have a look at what negotiation is. You may not have negotiated a wage before, but I bet at some point this week you have had to negotiate. If you have children, a spouse, a partner, parents, flat-mates or colleagues, I guarantee you have negotiated. Over this week I want you to jot down what you have negotiated. Write down who it was with, what it was for, whether you had to compromise and how you did that, or whether the negotiation failed and why. Note down how you felt before, during and after the negotiation and whether you would describe it as a good or bad negotiation.

By examining the small things we negotiate each day, we can build up a picture of our negotiation style and whether we can improve on it. Have a look back over your negotiation findings this week. Did you feel like each negotiation was steeped in conflict? Were voices raised, or threats used by the other party, or by you? There is no right or wrong at this moment; be honest with yourself; we are purely doing our research. You might have a way that you negotiate with children or your partner using threats as a negotiation tool, or compromising so that you both reach a happy agreement.

I want you to describe what you think a bad negotiation is. In as much detail as possible explain what you think would happen. You can choose what you want the two individuals to be negotiating; it might even be a story from your own experience. Make sure you give the story a beginning, middle and ending. Why did it go wrong, why would you describe it as a bad negotiation, how do both parties feel before, during and after the negotiation? Look back over what you have written and highlight the areas that make you feel most uncomfortable. Are you most uncomfortable reading about how people felt afterwards or during the negotiation?

Repeat the exercise, this time for a good negotiation. What makes this a good negotiation? How do both parties feel before, during and afterwards? Why do you think this is a good negotiation? Which parts are you going to highlight to show the best areas of the negotiation? Were they best at the beginning, middle, end or the whole way through? Why was that?

You should now have a picture of the areas of negotiation that make you uncomfortable, and the areas that you are happy with. This still doesn't mean you are ready to go out there and negotiate; it does mean that you can identify which areas you need to do some work on.

Sometimes we may not have to negotiate in person, but via email instead. Email can be a great or a terrible tool to use. I'm sure we can all remember receiving an email that made us uncomfortable, where something was lost in translation or else it was full of apologies.

Remember in the confidence section when we were looking at words that make you appear less confident in emails? These are the same words that you need to avoid when you are negotiating via email.

- Sorry	- But	- I'm no expert
- Just	- Try	
- Hopefully	- Actually	

To negotiate well, you need to be confident. By practising the skills we learnt in the confidence section, this will help you to negotiate. Emails can be powerful as you don't have to show that you are scared, embarrassed or shy. You can do your research and lay out your terms, what you are willing to negotiate for, or an amount of money you want to have. There is an art to negotiating via emails, and it goes like this:

Email 1

You have done your research. You know how much you want to make on this job, and the lowest you are willing to take. You see what benefits this work will bring to the Client and can back this up with your research, including statistics, testimonials, and previous clients experience of working with you.

You make your case for hiring you or your work at this price and explain the benefits they will gain from hiring you or your work.

(The price at this point is the highest price you would like to get for this job).

Before sending your email – scan for any of those negative words that make you appear less confident.

Email 2-The response

The new client/customer will either respond positively and accept your price, or more likely – they will say it is too expensive for them and start the negotiation. They should say why it is too costly, and if they are keen to have you and your work, they will offer something to negotiate with.

Email 3-Your response

As you have done your research about the client and have shown that there is a need for your work or else benefits from having your work – this is the moment to begin negotiating.

You would have given them your highest fee in the first email. We always start a negotiation high, so that we have somewhere to go. What you don't want to do here is drop to your lowest fee. What you want to do is begin to offer to remove some things in relation to that fee.

Your fee will be made up of transport costs, your time and some aspirational costs (I hope!) You can now offer to remove some of those costs only if your highest fee has some aspirational value and that the lowest price you are willing to take will still leave you with profit.

When I negotiate to run a course, I break it down as a price per student; I describe the extras they will receive (being added to my network for life), after support and workbooks for them to take away. I always add mileage and subsistence. Adding these allows me to remove the mileage and subsistence first. If it is still too expensive for them, I can offer to do the course for half a day instead, at a 20% discount, or else take more students without raising the costs – so instead of 20; I could teach 30 at the same price.

It is important to note, that I would have worked all of these offers out before I started the first negotiation email 1.

Email 4-Their reply

At this moment they will either agree, ask for more negotiation, or else say that they have to ask their superior/team etc. this is the moment you need to be strong.

One of the most powerful things you can do during a negotiation is to use silence. Silence gives you time to think; it also makes the other person feel like they need to fill the silence or offer something else. You don't want to be the person offering. During an email negotiation, there will be moments of silence. During one of my email negotiations, the person I was negotiating with said that they had to check with their superior. Four days passed before I heard from them.

Was I nervous during that time? Yes, I was. I knew though that I had to hold my nerve. If I had panicked and worried that I had asked for too much, I would have sent another email offering a worse deal for me, or checking that I hadn't offended them. If they are off to talk to their superior, this is a great thing. It means that they are serious about my offer and are now negotiating with their boss to be able to say yes to me. After the four days, they had the approval they needed and accepted my second offer.

Email 5-Your reply

Acknowledge that they need to check with their superior, team etc. and that you look forward to hearing from them this week, next week or soon.

Email 6-Their reply

They would either have received approval or not, which is the point when you need to either, lower your price further (still with profit), or make tangible changes to the lower rate, or be willing to walk away.

Email 7- Your reply

You can accept the offer (if it is right for you) and state clearly what the proposal includes, how you want payments to be paid with dates, timings, catch-up meetings, etc. attached to it. All of this becomes part of your written agreement and something useful to start using for all your work. It is less legally binding than a contract, but by setting out the terms of a formal agreement, it helps both parties understand what they have agreed. Plus if there are any problems along the way, you can refer back to the document to remind them what they (and you) decided before the work started.

If you are still negotiating at this point, make sure you don't end up without any profit. If you are lowering your price – tell them what you will have to remove to reach that price. Maybe they have to pay for the delivery of your artwork, or you have to reduce the number of students you can teach, or you will reduce the number of hours the course will run.

Email negotiation can sometimes take weeks. You need to be patient and hold your nerve. Be clear what they are getting for that price and be clear about what they lose from that price if they negotiate lower, and remember to state in your agreement and invoices, what the price includes. If it is a discount of 20%, make sure you say that on the invoice, so that next time you work with them they know, it was a reduced price. Time tends to alter people's memories. Unless you have stated the reduction somewhere, they will assume that the amount they paid all those months ago is the price you charge each time.

In every negotiation, whether in person or via email you need to work through the following points before you even start the negotiation:

Research

If you are already working for a company/client and have a track record of working for them, and you want to negotiate a raise, you need to do your homework. Look at the company's annual reports (you can find these online in the UK – a Google search should bring them up.) Is the company in a comfortable position so that they could pay you more? There is no point trying to ask for a raise if the company can't afford to give you one. Has the company improved its profits or customer feedback, based on the work you have done?

Keep a log of your achievements and positive feedback from each job you do. Put dates down and collect testimonials. All of this will put you in a stronger negotiating position. Did your art opening bring in more visitors to the town? Did the local shops have an increase in customers during that day? Ask them. Find out the facts that you can use. If you work for a company, can you get customer testimonials or prove an increase in the company's figures, profile, and awards based on the work you have done for them? Research is the most important thing you can do before a negotiation. It shows facts, (facts are hard to disregard), and it shows that you are valuable to that company or client.

Work out your figures.

What is your dream price? The price you dream of getting for your work. It might be a price that makes you slightly uncomfortable asking for it. (I sometimes call it 'the giggle price', an amount that makes you giggle when you say it, as it is pushing you out of your comfort zone). It is a price based on your long-term goals, your value, your work and your skills. You would add aspirational value into the mix as well. Remember that I told you I now charge 95% more than when I first started? This figure was my dream price. The first time I negotiated it was via email, I felt nervous, sick and uncomfortable asking for it the first time, even though I believed I was worth that amount and had the education and experience to prove it. I negotiated hard, and now I feel no panic, sickness or un-comfortableness asking for that amount again and again. The first time we do something it is always nerve-wracking, it gets easier each time we ask for it.

Once you have your dream figure, this is the figure you want to start with when negotiating. If you get it during your first round of negotiation give yourself a cheer; it proves that you did well, showed the research that proved you were worth that amount, and that you would deliver results for them.

The next figure you need to have is your mid figure; this is the figure that you would be most comfortable asking for. It is a figure you believe you are worth and still gives you a healthy profit for your time and work.

The last figure you need to have is the lowest. This figure still needs to have profit built into it as you can't negotiate to work for a loss. You also need to be happy to deliver the work for this price. There is no point feeling resentful when you have accepted a negotiated price. Better to walk away than say yes, if you feel like that.

Added extras.

Added extras are things you can use in a negotiation to reduce your fee by showing something tangible will be removed. It is always better to show that the figure is reduced due to removing something, rather than only reducing the fee alone. It shows the other person that the highest number was worth more because more came with it.

The types of extras that you can negotiate with are things like, benefits, feedback, installation costs, aftercare, long-term support or training. They can also include mileage, travel costs or subsistence. Giving these things a value allows you to remove them from the highest price and demonstrates to the client/customer that the high price came with added benefits for you (mileage/subsistence) or them (aftercare, installation etc.)

Hidden Benefits.

If you are already at a company or about to negotiate to work for a company before you settle your fee find out if there are any hidden benefits. These are benefits that you may not know about as they often don't' advertise them.

I had to negotiate a 6-month contract on a film once. I thought I got a good deal until I realised that I hadn't negotiated per diems when we were working away from the location. Per diems are extra money for meals including breakfast, lunch and dinner. I had unwittingly left hundreds of pounds on the table because I didn't know I could ask for them. The employer wasn't going to tell me that I could negotiate for them, as it was in their benefit for me not to have them. When I found out that my colleagues were receiving them and I wasn't, that fee I hadn't negotiated suddenly didn't look as good. Don't leave benefits you could have negotiated on the table. You could find out about holiday pay, half days off each month, gym membership, training, or mentoring? These are things that may have monetary value to you and can be part of your negotiation package if they won't accept your dream price.

When they say no.

You need to have already planned what you will do if they say no. Are you happy to negotiate to your lowest price? Are you comfortable achieving that price for the job? What is your plan B?

A plan B is something you need to have if they negotiate lower than your lowest price, or if the negotiation breaks down, and both parties can't reach a compromise. Sometimes this will happen, so you need to be prepared and know what you will do in that situation. Is there another job or client you can approach instead? Don't pin all of your hopes on one job or client. It can be a dangerous position to be in, as they may move, change their client base or go bankrupt. If this happens, you'll go down with them.

Try to have a plan B. Have another client you can approach,

have another job you can apply for, or another project you can offer them if they can't agree to the one you have presented them this time. Having a plan B puts you in a stronger position, as it means you aren't relying solely on them to provide you work; you can be stronger during the negotiation knowing that your life doesn't rely on this client or opportunity. Of course, this is easier said than done as we emotionally invest in everything we apply for. Having another option should release some of the pressure and make it easier to negotiate the price we would be happy with, and if we don't get it, be happy to walk away.

Always leave a negotiation on good terms. Agree to disagree, thank them for their time and that you look forward to meeting, working with them in the future. You never know when you will bump into them again. They may have a job in the future that you are more suitable for. By leaving on good terms, it keeps that door open for the future.

People might say no in many different ways. If you can practice what your response will be to the variety of no's – you will not only have an answer to the no, you will also feel calmer as it won't be such a surprise.

Here are five classic replies you may hear when you are negotiating.

1. "We can't afford it. That is the best offer we can do."

Your response should be based on the research that you have done. If you already work for this client or company you can talk about what benefits your work has brought for the company. Mention what profits the company made last year. Tell them what you have done for them and the company, and the results you have achieved and how you intend to build on them this year.

If you haven't worked for these people before, this is the point where you can begin to remove some of what you re offering. Say you can reduce your fee if you take away transportation, teach fewer students, or offer a payment plan for a piece of art – with interest or else no interest if you're feeling generous!

2. "That is more than someone in your position /role should earn."

Your response should again be based on your research if you already work for the company. Talk about the benefits and results you have achieved and ask if they changed your title it would then allow them to give you the x% more than you are asking for, based on the work you are already doing. If you are speaking to a new client ask them what they think would be an appropriate salary for someone performing at that level, or for a piece of artwork of that calibre. You can then say (based on your research) the hourly rate for someone in your role is x and it takes x number of hours to prepare for the service you are delivering or x number of hours to create the artwork. Remind them of the extra value you are offering based on your reputation, experience, talent etc. Often people are not aware of the time it takes to create something or the extra values that are built into the product or service.

3. If you have been offered the job/or the client is happy to buy your product, the negotiation for the fee/cost begins. They may say: "You're lucky to have this job in this current climate" or "You're lucky I'm making this purchase in this current climate."

Remind them that you haven't been offered a job because you are lucky, and they haven't wanted to buy your product because you are lucky. Those people chose you because you are the best candidate or because they love your product/artwork above everyone else. Remind them of the reasons why they have chosen you, your product, your service or your artwork.

4. "You're not experienced enough. That is what we pay people more experienced than you. You need to wait a while in the job before you earn that." Or "Your art isn't well known enough yet to command those fees."

When you are starting and building your career, profile or brand, you may hear this response when you start to sell your services or products/art. If you have looked at your pricing and correctly priced for your time, and overheads to get the 'base cost,' and have added what you feel is a correct aspirational amount, then you need to explain to them why you are experienced enough. Remember that experience doesn't need to mean having a PhD or be in business for decades. You have the skills and knowledge that no one else has. They may not be aware of all of your experience or abilities. You may have been building websites, products etc. since you were 12. Maybe you have taken workshops or been trained by well-known people in your field, or else you know how to work a specialist piece of software or have wonderful testimonials.

Remind them that you understand that pay is based on education, experience and accomplishments. Describe your accomplishments. They might be a previous project you created that brought in X amount in ticket sales or a piece of artwork that was featured in a magazine and the demand for your work increased by X%, or that you brought a project in under budget and saved a client X amount. Remind them why you are valuable now and not in three years, especially when you are starting or trying to add a chunk of aspirational value to your fee. These moments need some justification, both to the new client and customer, but also to yourself so that you believe in your value and have the confidence to ask for that amount.

5. "Your research is wrong. We are paying well for this job, product or artwork in today's market."

Put the onus back on them. Say that you are sure he or she has access to more resources than you do and ask them to share the data with you. You may hit a brick wall at this point, and need to negotiate other options; this is the moment to remove things like subsistence or offer a payment plan for your work. (Make sure you have a contract if you provide a payment plan so that you have a legal support structure if they don't make a payment or refuse to pay the last amount etc.)

If you do reach a brick wall and you have negotiated to your lowest fee, and they still won't accept it, you need to have a plan up your sleeve. Your most significant negotiation tool is the right to walk away. You need to have another client or customer you can approach instead. At the start of your career, this is harder; it is important not to accept work or money for your products, services and art that doesn't make you a profit or add to your reputation or network.

Sometimes we take work as a way to get more contacts, learn something, or reach new customers. Those can be valuable to your career, and it is essential to weigh up the pros and cons of taking that sort of work or accepting those sorts of clients. You need to know what other value you will gain if you are making a loss financially. We can't live off this sort of deal, so we need to understand that the benefits will create future income or clients for us.

Tip: If you are asked what you were paid in a previous job or for an earlier piece of art, you have the right to say that it is confidential.

Remember to review and update your skills audit. Those skills and experiences are sources of bargaining power. Is there a piece of software you know inside out that your client needs or do you have other contacts that you will bring to the table? All of these you can use in your negotiation to get the fee that you want.

Women tend to undervalue themselves and will start a negotiation too low. I've done this before, as I was worried about offending the other person or being too scared to ask for what I was worth. Once I had improved my confidence and believed in my worth, I stopped going in too low. Aim high when you begin a negotiation, as you will need to negotiate down from that point.

If negotiating in person makes you uncomfortable, make sure you talk slowly to buy yourself thinking time. Try to get them to name the figure first if you are applying for a new job/position. It is a lot easier to negotiate up from a number they have started with, rather than you handing over a figure and having to negotiate down. If there is a silence don't try to fill it. They will either be thinking about what you have said or else you want them to fill the silence. Rather than feeling uncomfortable, hold your nerve. Silence is the most powerful tool a woman can use when negotiating. We often panic and believe we need to fill the silence to make the situation more comfortable, or else we feel uncomfortable ourselves and so make a counteroffer before they have responded to the first one! Practice this with friends so that the silences don't feel so uncomfortable.

Start to think about your highest, mid, and lowest fees you want to charge for your work. If you are already about to sell some work, do some research, to back up your highest price. Remember to look back at your skills audit. Which of those skills could you use in your negotiation?

For the next month, I want you to practice the art of negotiation and record your findings. The trick to this exercise is to build up slowly. My brother in law always asks for a discount in shops or when booking hotel rooms. 90% of the time he does get a discount. Start with something small like asking for a discount when you buy something from a shop. I want you to get used to people saying no as well. The first time you receive a no you might feel embarrassed or uncomfortable, we want to practice receiving no's so that eventually they don't bother us as much.

My brother in law starts his discount hunting with the understanding that the other person will probably say no, and they also know to only ask for discounts from big companies or hotels that haven't sold all their rooms that weekend. A little research or an understanding of the situation the other person is in will go a long way to helping you have a positive negotiation. Try some of these out over the next month and built them up to more significant discounts. Record how you felt before, during and afterwards. What did they say? Did they offer any extras for the asking?

Here are some examples of things that you could try:

1. Negotiate for a day off or a treat you would like to have with your spouse, partner or flatmate.
2. Ask for a free pasty with your coffee if the café is near the end of the day. You know they will probably throw them out.
3. If you are buying several things at once, ask for a 10% discount.
4. If you are booking train/plane tickets, ask for a discount if you hire a car as well.
5. When booking a hotel, ask for a night free, or discount on dinner for your stay.

Come up with some of your own things you can practice negotiating with.

The key is to get no's some of the time so that no doesn't become a terrible proposition. I now actively love to haggle and negotiate for things. As long as I do it with humour and from a place of love (love of their product, hotel, scarf, coffee etc.), then we both enjoy that experience. I do my research and don't ask at a busy time, or when I know, they can't afford to give me a discount.

If you are uncomfortable about negotiating or asking for more wages, think about what you could do with that extra money. Would it allow you to help your family, your children or take further training? If it is hard to ask for yourself, imagine the people you could help with that money and do the negotiating for them. We can only help others when we have helped ourselves.

If you hear yes the first time you negotiate a fee – you are asking for too little!

Always remember that there are two of you involved in the negotiation. The other party will want something as well. Don't go for the jugular first of all. Be open, relaxed and confident. You have all of your research, a three-price tier structure, and a plan B up your arm.

If you both can't reach a compromise that is mutually beneficial, thank them for their time and walk away. You will hear no's. Rejection is all part of the freelance life and something we have to get used to. I find trying to enjoy the negotiation helps, and it is all good practice. Work out what you need and what you are willing to compromise before you enter the room, or send the first email. Remember you're Wonder Woman. You've got this!

11

Feedback

At some point in your career, you will receive or need to give feedback to someone. How this happens has a considerable amount of bearing on whether that feedback is received positively or negatively – even if it is good feedback!

Freelancers should actively hunt out feedback. It allows you to find out if what you are offering works, or has the desired effect you were hoping for. It allows you to find out if something was missing, and it will enable your clients and customers to give suggestions or praise you. Praise from clients and a customer helps you to build trust and attract new clients. We'll come back to this in more detail. First of all, I want us to understand how feedback works in the brain.

When we are approaching a new client or having an interview, at some point, the other person will give us some feedback. Not all feedback will be good, and it is essential to understand how to handle that.

The brain handles negative feedback information in different areas of the brain. Scientists have shown that negative emotions involve more thinking power, and the information is processed more thoroughly than positive ones. They now think that this was a survival instinct of our ancestors. By remembering a negative situation more clearly than a positive one it protected the tribe, and increased their chances of survival. It is why trauma is remembered more clearly than a day when not much happened, and you were happy.

Humans also tend to view people who say negative things as smarter. Depressing, I know, but also helpful. If we know that this is how we relate to negative feedback, or to people who say negative things, we can retrain ourselves safe in the knowledge that it is our brain wiring that is part of the problem.

The best way to give or receive negative feedback is one negative piece of feedback, followed by a positive bit of feedback.

They used to believe that the best way to receive negative feedback was good, bad, good. They called it the criticism sandwich.

They now believe that it doesn't work, as after a negative comment it increases brainpower, so what comes next is remembered in more detail. If you give a negative comment, then a positive, then a negative, the person is only going to remember the negative comments.

We can only retain and respond well to one negative comment at a time. We give more weight to critical reviews than positive ones. The best way to deal with this is to provide one negative comment, followed by a positive one. It means that we will remember the negative comment and the positive one, meaning that we are more likely to review the negative comment rationally as we know that we also received some positive feedback.

Have a look at this interview below. What is said and how would you respond to it?

Theatre owner:

We like your play.

We think it will fit in well with our holiday programme of events.

However, I don't have the time to deal with this right now.

What do you think they are actually saying?

Did you think that they were saying yes or no to your play?

What if I told you they were saying yes? They needed more help with finding the time to schedule, but they are interested. We could help them out by offering to help with scheduling, or working out when you could set up and take down the scenery so that you fit into their schedule. People are busy. They are not going to bring you in for an interview if they didn't like what you were offering.

They have said two positives about your play and one negative. Because the negative was delivered last, that is the part we latch onto. We forget or dismiss the positive points that came first.

This week I want you to notice when you give or receive feedback. If it is negative feedback did that person (or you) offer any positive feedback as well? When did they/you deliver the positive feedback? Was it before or after the negative feedback?

A week later what do you remember the most from the feedback? If you gave feedback, try to find out how that person felt about it a week later, and what they remember about the experience. (This isn't always possible, but if you can talk to them it will give you valuable knowledge.)

Having a look back at your results, is it the positive or negative feedback that you or they remember the most? Can you change the way you deliver one piece of negative feedback at a time? Track the results and see what the difference is.

By understanding how our brain works regarding negative feedback can help us to respond effectively. If we know that humans believe a person who uses negative comments more often, sounds more intelligent, we can re-educate ourselves to learn that this isn't true. Which in turn, empowers us in the workplace – as we know it is our brain's chemistry making us feel this way, rather than anything based on hard facts.

Learning how to receive negative feedback in the best possible way, will help you to deliver 'positive' negative feedback in the future. You want people to take on board what you are saying without swamping them with negativity so that they don't hear the positive feedback, or remember nothing at all.

Feedback is so useful for your career as a freelancer. If you ask for it well, it gives you invaluable knowledge that you can act on and improve. Feedback can also take the form of testimonials. Testimonials should be free to get, show that you have worked well for someone before, and they build trust so that others feel confident about hiring or buying from you.

There is etiquette involved in receiving testimonials. You need to think about the following things before you ask for them.

1. Did the client, customer have a good time or love the work you did for them
2. Have they worked with or purchased from you before?
3. Have you approached them for feedback?
4. Was it recently that you worked for them or they bought from you?
5. Have they recommended you to someone else?
6. Why would you want a testimonial from them?

Testimonials are time sensitive. You need to ask for them shortly after the work was completed, ideally within the same week. People have short attention spans and quickly forget the positive points that your work brought them. Creating a feedback form that you can send out helps you to act fast and efficiently. You need to ask them about the experience, what worked or didn't work for them. (Remember negative feedback helps you improve and grow.) Ask them what you did that would make them recommend you to a friend or new client.

Finally, ask them for a specific way that your work or product enhanced or changed their life (phrase these in your own words). Ask them if they are happy for their words to be edited down as a testimonial, and ask them to provide a photograph of themselves. Testimonials with photos attached are much more powerful. A picture helps us to identify with the person and builds trust. We can see that they are a *real* individual, not just a series of words.

The other thing you need to think about is how you will use your testimonials. Not all testimonials are created equal. Have a look at these examples below.

A. " I loved Stacey's bath product, and I would buy it again."

B. "Stacey's bath product is the best product for eczema prone skin on the market. After one week's use, my son's eczema has improved, and he is sleeping better at night for the first time in years."

C. "Claire gave an enlightening talk at the Cross Roads Conference. We would hire her again."

D. "Claire's talk at the Cross Roads Conference allowed me to identify gaps in my marketing plan. Since implementing the strategies, she set out; I have had a 20% increase in sales. I can't recommend Claire enough."

All of the testimonials are positive ones, but A and C give us very little information. If you were a new client or customer looking to hire someone for a job or to make a purchase would A and C testimonials make you do that? Although they are positive, they don't contain much knowledge or results that I would use to make an informed decision before hiring or purchasing from them. You need testimonials to work for you on two different levels.

Level one – they need to show that by hiring or buying from you, this produced tangible results that helped them or solved a problem.

Level two – they need to build trust between you and future clients and customers. The way to do this is by presenting facts.

If you receive a testimonial similar to A or C, you weren't asking the right feedback questions. Think about how you want to use your testimonials first. Are they to be used on paper, on a website, as part of marketing literature? What message would you want to convey on all of those platforms? What points or facts do you want new clients or customers to know? What types of questions would you ask a previous customer or clients to describe those points or facts?

Be specific in the way you ask for feedback. Asking them if they would use you again only gives you a yes or no answer. You want to use what journalists called open questions. These are questions that encourage the person to tell you more than yes or no. Here are some examples of open questions:

A. Can you describe the results you have experienced after taking the course?
B. What types of results have you felt after using my product?
C. How did you feel after taking part in the dance class?
D. Can you describe how the artwork has changed the environment in your home?

Open questions should prevent one-word answers. Of course, there are always exceptions to the rules. Plan what open questions you would ask to gain three testimonials from previous work you have done. Use these over the next week to collect three testimonials from past clients and customers. It doesn't matter if only friends and family have purchased from you at this moment, you can still use them as testimonials while your business/career grows.

Think about where you will use the testimonials, what you want them to say and why, how, you want new customers and clients to respond to them. Then create a feedback form you can use to collect future testimonials.

To help with this, have a look around at competitors and see if they use testimonials. Where do they put them? How do you respond to them? Are they giving you enough information? Do they make you want to purchase from that person? Do they feel trustworthy?

You can make notes about the messages they convey and then work out how you would ask an open question to receive a testimonial like that.

Have fun with them and collect as many testimonials as you can. You don't have to use them all at once, and it is a good idea to change and update them during the year, or for specific projects or launches.

12

Legals

B efore I dive into this section, I want to make sure you understand that I am not a legal representative, nor am I here to give you legal advice. I have noted points where it is useful to get help from a legal expert so that you protect yourself and your clients.

At some point in your career, you have to start acting like a professional. I like to call it 'going pro.' We usually begin our career from a place of passion. There is something that we are interested in, and we enjoy working on it every day. We then wonder if we could build a career, and earn income from it. It is a rare individual who looks at the creative industries and chooses the one they think will make them the most money. I have met those individuals, but it isn't the way that I like to work.

Passion has pros and cons. The passion drives us, helps us get up in the morning to do our work. It keeps us going through the hard times, and encourages others to hire or join us. Keeping that in mind, you can become passionate about the business side as well. I've heard countless excuses from creatives that they are no good at figures or dealing with the paperwork, but then they manage to organise the logistics for an international exhibition, and everything runs smoothly.

I believe that if you know how to use a diary, then you are intelligent enough to understand business basics. This chapter is about 'grown-up time.' You might find it uncomfortable, or want to hide under the duvet, but stay with me, as I believe that knowing the facts can empower you. By understanding the basics of what you need to do, you can plan or ask for help. Not knowing or understanding is a scary place to be.

The things that I am going to talk about now apply to the UK. These things change frequently based on government and council policies. It is easy to check for updates online.

Let's start at the beginning. When we move from a hobby to earning money for our products or services we need to register as self-employed. At this point, you have entered 'grown-up time' and started 'Going-pro'. It is the moment you stop playing and start being professional. Going self-employed often scares creatives. Be excited about it! You are taking the first step on the career ladder of your creative career. Of course, there are certain things you have to do when you are self-employed, and rules and regulations that you have to follow. They aren't complicated, and there are many people, websites and software that can help you.

At its basic level, being self-employed means being responsible for your income, sick pay, pension and tax. (That's the grown-up version.) You can also look at it as taking control of your career, destiny, timetable, holidays and the right to take the whole winter off if you feel like it. When you are dealing with the grown-up stuff, it is good to remind yourself of all of the benefits as well. When your friends have a couple of weeks off a year, and you can decide if you work when it's sunny, remember these moments. They will help you to get through the paperwork.

Once you have registered to be self-employed online, they will send you a unique code that is yours for the whole of your self employed career until you decide to go back to employment or change the status of your company to Ltd or corporation. (More on that later.) Keep this code safe, as you will need it every time you log on to do your tax returns.

The next system that you want to put in place is a way to collect all of your receipts, mileage and permissive expenses. I've met countless creatives who are misinformed about receipt keeping. You do need to keep a receipt for every purchase you make for your business. It does need to show the details and date of where you bought something, where possible. If the receipt doesn't list what you bought, then you can write it on the receipt. Even if you are inputting the information onto accounting software, you will need to keep our receipts for seven years. Yes, seven! It made my mind boggle too when I first found out. In case you get audited, you keep those receipts. That basically means the tax office comes and checks through all of your accounts. It is much more painful than that, as it takes up days of your time and you can lose income during that period. Having clear and well-ordered accounts will help if you ever find yourself audited.

Tip: The FSB – Federation of Small Business – charge about £175 a year for membership. What is great about them is that the membership includes insurance for loss of earnings in case you are audited. They also offer free legal advice and keep you up to date with policy and tax changes. I like to think of them as your 'phone a friend' when you have a business or legal question.

The way that I dealt with my accounts when I was a self-employed, sole trader was by pinning clear envelopes in monthly amounts and dropping in all of my invoices and receipts for that month. At the end of the month, I sat down and worked through them, putting them into a spreadsheet, numbering and filing all the receipts. It might sound painful, and there is lots of software that you can now use that helps with this process like Kashflow or Xero. I use Kashflow, as it is what my accountant uses, so it makes the process easy.

It doesn't matter what system you use, as long as you have a system. When you first register for self-employment status in the UK, the government offers you free workshops in bookkeeping and accounting so that you start off understanding what you can, and cannot put against expenses. A good accountant will be able to tell you this as well.

I'm not going to go into any more detail about self-employment as there are plenty of more qualified accounts and government officials who can help you, and I'm not a legal expert. I want you to remember that if you behave like a professional at the beginning, people are more likely to take you seriously.

These days everyone needs a website. It is your shop window, portfolio, a CV that people can read, and decide to hire you from. Without having a website it is hard for new clients and customers to find you, but also to check if you are trustworthy, have done great work before, and have testimonials from happy clients to prove that you have. Having a website comes with some legal responsibilities. The government often changes their digital legal requirements, so it is vital for you to check what they are and keep up to date with those policies. Here are the basic legal things you need to include when building your website (do check to make sure there aren't new ones):

DIGITAL LEGALS

1. Cookies.

Cookies aren't only delicious things to eat. They can be small pieces of software that land on a person's computer or mobile device when they view a website. They help with some of the functions of the site, and they can also fill up someone's computer. It is now a legal requirement for people to say that they accept your cookies before continuing to view your website. You may have seen cookie policy pop-ups or tabs saying cookie policies on people's websites. You have to include this on your site to remain legal. A web developer can help you with this.

2. Terms and Conditions

At the bottom of web pages, you'll see the terms and condition tabs. These are terms and conditions people have to abide by for using someone's website. They may also include the terms and conditions of buying a product from them online. They can add things like a refund policy and delivery times as well. If you sell a service, they can let the person know that you cannot guarantee results or revenue for using your service. Have a look at some of your competitors' terms and conditions. What have they listed? Have they missed out something that you would want to include?

What you mustn't do is copy someone's terms and conditions and pass them off as your own. They are legal documents, and you may not be aware of what you agree to. Lawyers can be expensive. The way I did it, was to write my Terms and Conditions and then have a lawyer check it for me. It meant I only paid for an hour of their time and was safe in the knowledge that the Terms and Conditions were right for my business and me.

3. Emails

If you contact clients, customers or fans via email, and send out newsletters to their email addresses, there are some legal requirements you need to be aware of. You cannot add people to an email list without something called double-opt-in. (This is a legal requirement in Europe and Canada.) Double opt-in means that a person signs up to your email newsletter. Then they receive an email asking them if they definitely wanted to sign up, and check they added their email address to the list. They say yes, and then they receive an email thanking them for signing up and explaining how they can unsubscribe from the list whenever they want to. Every other email or newsletter that you send them, from the list they have signed up to, must include an unsubscribe link at the bottom. If this sounds too complicated, there is free software like MailChimp, which can set this up for you.

In Mailchimp you link it to a sign-up form on your website. Someone enters their details, and then Mailchimp forwards them the opt-in and Mailchimp sends them the thank you email you created on Mailchimp. It is smart software as it includes the recipient's name on the email, which makes it more personal. You don't have to do anything apart from writing one thank you email. MailChimp includes template versions if you aren't confident about writing our own, and has a free version for up to 2000 monthly subscribers. Other companies offer similar software.

5. Data Protection and GDPR.

The law relating to emails has also changed recently, and you must now comply with GDPR rules. At a basic level, this means you have to follow the double-opt-in rules, and you also have to have systems in place to protect those people's information and make it available to them if they request it; this has come on the back of hackers accessing large companies data. It isn't enough for you to hold them on a word document.

Whenever you collect someone's email address, personal details or payment details you have to comply with data protection. Data protection is updated regularly, and it is your responsibility to keep up to date with the changes. Data protection at its basic level means that you agree to protect the information and personal details that the person has given you.

Knowing what policy changes are coming up will help you to prepare for them. In the digital age, we cannot get away from technology. Even if all of our work is hands-on using paint and clay at some point, you will have to send an email or create an online gallery for your work to reach new customers. Knowing the rules will help you to behave professionally from the start, to put systems in place and to prepare for any policy changes. A good web developer should be up to date with all of the changes and can help you apply them to your website.

6. The identity of your business.

You are legally required to identify yourself and your business on your website. By that, it means that you must include the following somewhere on the site for people to find if they require it:

Your company name (or your own name if you are a solo freelancer).

If your company is registered as an Ltd company or partnership, you need to state the address of where it is registered, which might be your home address.

- You also need to include the company registered number.
- You need to have your postal address and the company email address available for people to find.
- If you are VAT registered, you also need to include this, even if your website isn't an online shop.
- It is also good practice to have a photograph of you as well.

7. Accessibility

Accessibility is the one area that many websites fail. People aren't aware that it is a legal requirement under the Equality Act of 2010, to add accessibility elements to your site.

At a basic level it means that you must include the following:

- Include an accessibility statement on the website.
- That you include people with disabilities in user research when building the site.
- That if there is video content you provide transcripts or subtitles for those who are unable to hear- this is the same for podcasts.
- Your site needs to work on the most commonly used assistive technologies like screen magnifiers.

Some of these you might not be able to have at the moment, but it is essential to know that they are a legal requirement and to check that you are up to date with them.

Now we have dealt with the basic digital legal requirements we can move onto the other legal things you need to think about when you turn professional.

1. Insurance.

If you interact with the public in any way, you will need to have public liability insurance. Even if the people only come once a year to your open studio day, you need to make sure that if a painting were to fall off the wall and hit them, that you are covered. Many companies offer specialist public liability insurance for artists, coaches and dancers. Make sure it includes cover for all activities like workshops, gallery installation etc.

AN (artists newsletter) magazine offers public liability with their yearly membership. Their membership is only £38 per year, or £16 for a student (2019), which is a fantastic bargain when most public liability insurance is over a hundred pounds per year. They also cover you for workshops and galleries. Do check the small print before signing up and make sure that it applies to everything you want to do.

2. Contracts and agreements.

No matter whether you have only started your career/business, you need to think about contracts and agreements from day one. Contracts and agreements protect you, your career and business. Even if you are only paid for a couple of hours work you did for someone, I would still consider using a contract or agreement. The difference between contracts and agreements is a legal one. Contracts are legally binding and will hold up in a court of law, agreements are still legally binding, but they don't hold as much weight as a contract.

When you put a contract together for a job, you set out the agreement you made between you and a client. It would state the work that you had agreed to complete, the time frame, any extra requirements, and what the job is - (in detail) – and the cost of extras such as re-writes, re-designs, or additional classes. By clearly telling the client or customer what they have agreed to, there is less chance of miscommunication. It also protects the client or customer, because if you don't' deliver everything you have promised, then they have a right to challenge you, and in the worst case scenario take you to court in breach of contract.

Don't let this put you off using them. Agreements can be written in a more informal way to a contract, and they can help you if someone is late paying or starts to add lots of extra requirements long after you started the job. You can refer back to the agreement in these scenarios, and remind them what they agreed to for the fee, or that late payment has charges added. What you decide to include in your agreements is between you and your clients. It is a good idea to make a master template that you can use again, and again; this will allow you to adjust it for each client without having to create an entirely new one each time.

3. Model Releases

If you are a photographer, filmmaker and use models and locations in any publicity photographs you need to obtain a signed model/contributor/location release form. Whenever you record a person onto film or video, they have to understand how and when you intend to use their image. If they are a minor, their parent or guardian would need to sign and agree to the model release on their behalf. Sometimes locations need a release as well for you to be able to use the image/footage of them. You would get the owner or guardian of the location to sign a location agreement. Sometimes this is impossible to police like the Eiffel Tower in Paris, which is protected by copyright and no images or footage of it can be used without a licence. I'd challenge you to look online at how many items come up with the Eiffel Tower printed on them, and I guarantee you that they haven't all obtained a licence to use the Eiffel Tower! Even illustrators can be challenged under these copyrights laws. I believe this is where it all gets a bit ridiculous. I campaigned for this not to happen to the London Skyline. It is a battle we are still fighting, as it would mean that any image taken in London of certain skyline buildings, would be subject to copyright by the owner of the building. In one sweep it would jeopardise the whole of the UK photojournalism community. Despite all of my feelings about this topic, if you are filming or photographing on private property (some parks are private), you need to obtain a location agreement if you wish to use the images or footage professionally. In the same way that a model release works – you are getting the owner to agree to you using their image for your work. Remember; don't copy one from someone else online! As with contracts you can't replicate this as it is a legal document and you need a lawyer to create one for your requirements. Once you have created one, you can adapt it and use it again and again.

With all of these documents, make sure you get them signed by all parties before the work starts. I've heard of cases of television companies filming documentaries and then trying to get the contributor release signed at the end, and the contributor deciding that they weren't going to sign it. Not signing made the footage un-useable and wasted everyone's time and money. Protect yourself, and your clients before problems arise. In the long run contracts and agreements will make you appear more professional, which is particularly important when you are starting.

Make a list of the areas you need to think about to make your business professional and secure. These could include agreements, data protection on your website, or GDPR compliance and mailing lists. These things only need to be set up once and then updated when necessary. Getting it right from the start will protect you in the long run. Beginning as a professional will help you to believe in yourself, and in turn, it will build confidence in your abilities when interacting with clients and customers. Begin as if you are a successful business then others will believe you are, and eventually you will be, with hard work, luck and patience.

13

Social Media

Whether we love or hate it, social media has become an essential part of any creative career. The easiest way to deal with it is to work out how much time and energy you (or a member of staff) can donate to it, and on which social media platforms your target customers and clients interact. What I don't want you to feel is overwhelmed by it all. I'm going to explain strategies and time-saving devices that should make it simple to use and update without much effort.

When I was starting, I thought I had to be on every social media account. I had twitter, Tumblr, Flickr, Pinterest (I was one of the original 5,000 to test Pinterest), Instagram, several Facebook accounts – groups and pages, Whats- app, Snapchat, Google+ YouTube channel. Sounds exhausting, doesn't it?

I was putting posts up when I felt like it or thought of something. I replied to comments sporadically and felt overwhelmed that no one was interacting or reading anything I posted. If this sounds familiar, I'm going to help you work out when and what you should be posting, how often, and on what platforms. Social media should be fun. It's there to find out more about our industry, what your clients and customers like, share good news, and collect feedback. It is the most powerful marketing tool you can have and can cost nothing, apart from a few hours of your time once a week.

First I want to show you how the rules have changed so that you understand the impact social media and the Internet has had, and why you need to be part of that movement.

Some of the most successful businesses on the Internet have broken all of the moulds.

- UBER is the biggest taxi company in the world but owns no cars.
- Facebook is the biggest content provider in the world but creates no content.
- Ebay is the world's biggest store but owns no physical shops.
- Air b n b is the biggest hotel/room provider in the world but own no real estate.

They have all broken the rules of what we once thought was possible. Rather than being scary, I find this exciting. It means that millions of people, from their bedrooms, can now create worldwide marketing campaigns and connect with new customers and clients without getting out of their pyjamas. The Internet and social media are still so young, which means that you have the right to mould a place in that world as well. In some ways, we have entered the future, and in other ways, I think we have gone back in time.

One hundred years ago we shopped very differently to the way we do now. We used to go to the local store where they knew our name, knew our family, knew what we liked and what we bought last week. They were able to make personal recommendations based on what they know you liked or disliked. You also knew all about them. They were part of your community. You knew if they had had a good week or not and you knew if they had recently been on holiday. I believe that we have gone back 100 years in terms of customer service. I think this is a good thing. We know whom we are buying from or hiring, we know what their background is, we know if they like to do the same things we do. They also know what we love, and can recommend, or offer us discounts if we have bought from them before. Social media has made you the community shopkeeper. To be successful in this media world, you need to think like that shopkeeper, and believe that all of your customers are part of your community.

So how do we communicate with our community in a meaningful way? How do we offer or show them things that might be of interest to them? How do we make them feel like a welcomed member of the community? We need to go back and have a look at the customer profiling that we did. Have a look at what you wrote down. What did your customers and clients like to do with their time? What time did they go or come back from work? Did they commute or work from home? You can add much more detailed questions to your customer profiling as you begin to build a picture of them. If you struggle to imagine what their life is like, you can interview past customers or ones that you are hoping to do business with.

You are now going to build up a social media marketing customer profile. You need to think about the times of day they will be on social media. Do they wake up and check Facebook while lying in bed? Do they look at Twitter on their way to and from work? Once the kids are in bed, do they scroll through Pinterest and Instagram? Do they only look at social media in the week or the weekend?

You may not know all of these answers as you're not your client or customer. The best way to find out is to ask them. You can do a quick survey or have a look online when your clients are most active on the platforms you want to use, or look at how your competitor's customers interact with them. You can only make social media marketing effective when your clients and customers see it. Otherwise, you are effectively putting all of that content you have created straight into a bin that no one will ever see.

Before we look into what you need to be writing for content, I want to talk about how much you should be creating and how much you should be interacting with or sharing and reposting. Write down in as much detail as possible what you currently do on social media. Which platforms do you use? What sort of content do you write? How often do you write content? What time of day do you post? Then write down how much time you would be happy to dedicate to social media marketing each day or week. You might not want to do it at all; so whom could you hire to help you?

Once you have an idea of the times of day your customers and clients interact with social media, you can plot out what would be the best times of day for you to post. I know that my audience usually gets onto Facebook during their lunch hour, or at 3 p.m. when they begin to have a work slump and want some distraction. 3 pm also means that my audience in America has woken up, and they are looking at social media before they head to work. I also know that my Instagram followers are only going to be looking when they get home from work, the kids are in bed, or it's the weekend. My twitter followers, on the other hand, will mainly be checking their feed during the commute to and from work. What you are starting to see is a social media interaction graph. I will call it an SMI. It allows me to know when I need to be interacting and when I need to be silent.

I will talk about the type of content you should be posting in a moment. First I want you to understand the percentage of your content that will be seen, even if you are posting at the right time of day for your audience. You'll be surprised at how little it is. Facebook, for example, only 2% of all content is seen. That means that 98% of what you post has the potential to go into that social media bin no-one ever looks in. Don't feel disheartened, as there is a way around this. You want to create content that is going to be useful for your audience. Try to make sure each piece of content you post has a call to action. A call to action encourages the audience to interact with you and your posts. It can be something simple like asking them to comment below, to click a link taking them back to your website or asking them a question that they answer in the comments. You can also ask them to share the content.

TIP: Limit calls to action to one per post. People get confused if you ask them to do several things at once. Your call to action needs to be clear, simple and something that they can do immediately.

Think of some calls to action that you have responded to. What did they ask you to do? Why do you think they wanted you to take that action? Could some of those types of calls to action work for your audience?

Have a look back at how much time you said you would be willing to give to social media marketing each day or week. Be honest with yourself. You don't want to promise to do something and then wear yourself out by having to create content rather than your creative work. What if I told you that you could write all of your content for the next two weeks in a couple of hours and only have to post it once?

Automating as much of your business as possible will help you to have more time to create your creative work and bring in income. There are platforms available for you to use for free for up to three social media accounts, to schedule all of your social media content. A quick internet search will help you find some for your preferred platform.

The way that I schedule my content is that on a Tuesday morning I look through all of the newsletters and articles I have ever saved over the previous week; these all get funnelled into an email folder for me to look at in one go. At the moment I don't have time to create all of the content myself. I also enjoy sharing articles that I know my community will find interesting. Others might say that this could lead them to my competitors if they click on an article that I haven't generated, which might be the case for a few, but I feel secure that my community will keep returning to me as I provide them more than a few articles.

Once I have sifted through all of the articles that I want to share with my audience, I load them into a scheduling platform and write a post above the article about why I have found this interesting, how it relates to my work or their work, and finally I finish the post with one call to action. I usually share articles a couple of times. If I have a new blog post or podcast I want to share, I will repost this about five times across the week with a slightly different copy (text). I then set the posts to schedule for the times and days that I know my audience will be interacting with that social media platform.

There is so much to learn about social media that I would need to write a whole new book about it, as it is updated all the time. Keep an eye on what your competitors are doing, and learn from them.

Be careful with your mental health and social media. It can become all-consuming, and I know from personal experience that you feel like you need to be on it 24/7 and worry when you don't have enough followers. It is essential to take breaks if you need them and come back to social media another time. You can be honest with your audience, if they are the right customers/ clients for you, and let them know the reasons why you are taking a break. People are more open to digital-detox breaks, and I hope that it is something you will think about for the future.

There are lots of rules and formulas out there that talk about how much you should be posting. The average rule of thumb is to be writing your own content 30% of the time. Then 70% of the time you should be commenting and interacting with other people's content. (This changes to 20 x 80 on Twitter.) If all of that brings you out in a hot sweat, remember to go back to the beginning and think about what it is you want to achieve on each of the social media platforms you have chosen. If it is to sell a product, review how your competitors are successfully selling on those platforms. If it is to gain new clients and customers, go back to your customer profiling and work out when they are most active on those platforms. Constantly review what is or isn't working, and adjust your social media marketing plan to accommodate those changes.

The other place that you should think about adding your business, or a page about your career- is Google maps. If you want to appear high up in the Google ranks it makes sense to put yourself on one of their platforms. It's a simple process to register. They send a code to the address that you have listed to prove that it is you. Enter the code into the URL they send you, and then you appear on Google maps. For you to see star ratings next to your listing you need to have five reviews, (less than five reviews (even if they are all 5-star ratings) means that they won't show up in the listing).

These are all simple and free things that you can do to make yourself appear professional to the outside world. I always believe that it is best to start as you plan to go on. Look at your web presence, social media, and branding. Think about how you look to other companies and professionals. I bet that you usually do an Internet search before you buy or hire someone or buy something. Think about whether you read reviews or not before you make purchases. Would your customers or clients do the same for you? You have begun to build up a social media picture of your customer and clients.

I am now going to help you to plan a month's worth of content; this doesn't have to be hard. Without overthinking it, write down a list of 40 topics that you think would interest your customer or clients. Is there a problem that you can help them solve or something that you think they will find inspiring? Maybe there is an event or anniversary that relates to what you are selling or teaching? Out of the 40 circle 30 that interest you the most. Can you write a post of about 300 words around that topic, or record a five-minute video on your phone, to share with your audience/clients about it? Thirty topics would allow you to send out a post nearly every day of the week, which gives you a month's worth of content for social media or your website. If you get stuck for ideas, ask your customers/ audience what they would like to hear or learn from you. Content doesn't have to be complicated.

The last area to think about is the platform LinkedIn. I don't recommend this for everyone, as it can seem very business oriented, but you might be surprised to learn that the fashion industry uses it regularly to find new staff. Look at how your industry uses it. LinkedIn also has groups that you can join. The groups relate to topics that might be of interest to your business or career. You can participate in the conversations or ask questions. It's a great way to build up an online community and support in your field. You can also share posts on it, as you would for Facebook.

To make it easier for people to find you, and see what you do, it is essential to fill in your profile completely. Make sure you ask previous clients or customers for endorsements in the same way that you would use testimonials on your website. You can also ask for evidence of skills. You list which skills you want to be known for, and then LinkedIn asks your followers to recommend you for those skills. It is another way of building trust and evidence for new clients and customers. It proves that you own those skills and have used them to a professional standard.

Don't think of LinkedIn as only a place to hold your CV. It is so much more than that. It allows you to network in your field and build contacts. By joining groups, you can network and connect to people higher up in your industry. You can view the profile of someone you want to connect to and see which groups they are a member of and then join those groups.

One way to make sure your profile is found quickly (and look more professional) is by changing the URL of your Linkedin profile. Currently, when you join, it appears as a long run of numbers. You can change it to your name instead. So your LinkedIn URL would look like this http://www.LinkedIn.com/in/yourname

There are lots of help pages on the Internet that will talk you through how to do this.

List Building

The last part of your social media package is List Building. You may not have heard of list building, but this is the most robust way to build your relationships with new and exciting clients and customers.

List building at its basic level is someone giving you their email address with permission for you to send them things that will be of interest to them.

Here are the financial reasons why you should be list building:

For every $1 you spend on an email you have the potential to earn $37 back.

For every $1 spent on banner ads on platforms like Facebook, you have the potential to earn $2.

Email campaigns are like going to the bank with a pound and coming out with close to forty pounds! Nothing else converts like that.

I hate the word newsletter, but it is the easiest way to describe what list building is. By getting old and potential clients and customers to sign up to your list, you can directly send them content, offers and news about your career/business that they will be of interest to them. It is the best way to direct market to those that are already interested in what you are doing. The rule of thumb is to share content that they would find exciting and useful 80% of the time, and then sell 20% of the time.

There are lots of platforms that you can use to create newsletters. I personally like MailChimp, but many other platforms do the same thing. Have a look at them and work out what is best for you. MailChimp offers a free platform up to 2000 monthly subscribers to your list. You can create a master template uploading your logo and images. Alternatively, if you prefer to send a text email only, this option is available. It allows you to schedule when the email/newsletter goes out, and it also allows you to segment your list so that you can send things to different people. I do this when I want to let people on my list know that an event is coming to their area. Not everyone on my list is from the UK, so it would be pointless me telling someone in Australia that there is an event being held in London next week.

One of the features that I find most useful is that you can track how many people open your emails, whether they clicked on any links, and who they are; which helps you to work out what is or isn't working.

I want to help you now to come up with a month's worth of content that you can send out in emails. Before you do this, sign up for Creative Women International's mailing list at www. CreativeWomenInternational.com/resources to have a look at the thank you letter, and the free download that you receive for signing up. Would the download make you sign up or that you have the chance of being the first to hear about offers and events? This week have a look at any other email lists that you have joined. What was the subject line of the emails that you opened? Why did they make you open them? Sign up to another list that you are interested in, and examine how they communicate with you in terms of the language they use or offer they give you. Write all of this detail down as this is the best way to build up a picture of what may or may not work for you, your clients and customers.

Next, we are going to write down ten emails' subject headings that would make you open an email. Think about the ones that you have opened in the last month. Out of those ten headings choose four that you can create an email or create content around. Over the next month sign up to something like MailChimp and begin to build your list by getting people to sign up. Create an opt-in, like a help sheet they would find useful. Send out one newsletter/email a week with content that will interest them, and if you are not sure what that is, ask them questions about problems they need help solving.

Tip: Remember to set your email up so that it is GDPR compliant. You can do this on platforms like MailChimp.

Forty-eight hours after each campaign is sent out, have a look at the statistics for each campaign and see how many people have opened it or not. Things disappear down people's email list; I know this from experience as my inbox can have over a thousand emails in it day to day. Don't feel bad about sending it out to them again. They may have missed it, and are glad that you sent it again. By the end of the month, you should begin to see what is or isn't working. Anything over 40% engagement means you are doing very well.

The key with all of this is making it work for you, with minimal effort for excellent results. Make sure you review everything you are doing and adjust if something doesn't work. It is only by testing things can we discover what works or not.

14

Finding New Clients And Audiences

Finding new clients and customers is the lifeblood of your business. Be careful not to neglect those customers and clients who got you where you are today. It can take seven times more work to gain a new client or customer than it does to find a new one. So before you run off to find the shiny new customers and clients, I want you to have a look at the ones you have already worked with. Can you open up a dialogue about new work, can you give them a discount for being a loyal customer or can you offer them something before you share it with the wider world? We have all been customers in our lifetime. Think of the times when you had felt cared for or rewarded by a company or person when you made a purchase. Did they make you feel like you were part of a caring community; did they offer you a gift as part of the package or a VIP invite to an event?

In the customer profiling section, I asked you to think about all the times that you had fantastic treatment as a customer. This time I want you to think about whether they made you feel special or not. It doesn't have to be an online experience. It could be when you arrived late at a hotel, and they still managed to rustle you up a sandwich from the kitchen, or a train company you booked tickets from gave you a 20% discount on all future travel, as a thank you for being a loyal customer.

Think about all of the details. Had you purchased or hired from them before? Was it a surprise what they did for you? Did you use the discount or gift that they offered you? Did you tell others about your experience? How did it make you feel at the time? How do you think about that company or individual now? Have a look back at your answers. Is there something here that you can implement in your own business/career?

Adding benefits doesn't have to cost you more. Remember that it is seven times more work to gain new customers and clients. That's a lot of work costs in hours for you. Spending some time on the ones you already have will save you money in the long run. You can also increase the price of your products or services to be able to offer great packages or experiences for your customers. That might sound counterintuitive- I'll explain how it works.

There is a double-glazing window company where I live. They are family run and have a good reputation. There are other family-run window companies in the area as well that have a good reputation and are cheaper. The most expensive one is the one that is the busiest. No one talks about how expensive they are, what they talk about is the fantastic customer service and the aftercare package that each customer gets whether they have bought one window or a whole house full. By being more expensive, they can deliver that after sales package, yet that after sales package is what attracts customers and makes them pay more!

There is a glossy magazine that covers fashion, international affairs and design. They offer a subscription service to have the magazine delivered to your door. Most subscription services offer you a discount for paying in advance for the magazine. Quite often it is a substantial discount of about 40% off the retail price. They also entice you with a gift for signing up. This magazine is different. They do offer a gift of a stylish bag to carry your magazine in, but the subscription price costs more than if you went to the shop to collect it yourself. Surprised? I was.

They give you access to their digital archive of back issues but aren't the only magazine to offer this. What they are providing is the magazine delivered to the door of their customers without the hassle of going to the shop to buy it themselves. They know that most of their customer base is made up of international business people, the types of people who are busy making money or flying all over the world to meetings. They don't have time to pop to the shops when the latest issue comes out. They are willing to pay more to make sure it arrives on their doorstep than to sign up for a discount. They have funds and don't need to worry about saving 40% of the sale price. This magazine knows this, and so they charge them for it. Sure, there is a stylish bag that comes with the subscription (which is also great advertising for the magazine as it has their name on it), but it is the magazine delivery that means more to their client.

Go back and have another look at your customer profiling. What other things are they interested in that you could use to give them extra value? What were their hobbies, or where they went on holiday? Were they short of time like the magazine subscribers? Can you make their life easier or more fun by offering them something extra? Have a look at your customer profiling and pull out three areas that you could expand on. Think about three things you could provide for your clients and customers.

Don't worry about the cost of delivering this at the moment only think about the idea.

If you get stuck, have a look at what things you valued as a customer when someone gave you excellent service, a discount or a gift. Once you have come up with your three ideas choose one that you would like to try out. How much extra would it cost you? How much extra would you need to add to your fees to offer this? What you don't want to do is find yourself out of pocket.

Remember I talked about my fees going up 95% since I started valuing what I was offering? I don't deliver the same service that I did before. My clients get bonus's, aftercare packages and constant contact with me if they need it. All of that takes up my time and money. The only way I can deliver that service is by increasing my fee. No one minds as they feel like they are getting excellent service and are happy to pay for it. I wouldn't have dared raise my prices by 95%, without extras, and neither should you. You need to build trust, reputation, and aspirational value before you can jump up a pay scale.

If you have been in the business for a while, you could start by offering gold, silver and bronze packages. There will always be someone who wants a bargain (they may not be your ideal customers, or you may want to make sure you don't exclude them if they can't afford more, but have been very loyal.) You can offer them a bronze service that gives them the basic package of what you are providing, the silver service will provide them with some extra benefits, and the gold service should make them feel like a VIP. When we are scared to increase our prices, we worry we might lose valuable clients and customers. It can be useful to explain what they are gaining from the new fee structure – or allow them the chance to buy something at the bronze price, clearly stating what they get for that and that any extras will take them onto the silver package. Most people are very understanding when you explain why your prices are rising. Communication and honesty are the only way you can successfully run your career.

Now that we know how to look after the customers and clients we already have, we can move on and think about how to attract new ones. I'm going to talk about customer profiling during most of this section. Having those notes with you is essential. Knowing where your ideal customer hangs out and spends their time is half the battle won. What you don't want to find yourself doing is a massive marketing campaign in lots of places that your client or customers may not ever visit or see. By trying to talk to everyone, we end up talking to no one. Being clear about your customer profiling will save you money and time in the long run.

A great way to start is by asking your existing clients and customers where they found you. You can offer them the chance to win a free product or part of your service if they answer a few questions about your business. Some of their answers might surprise you. Was it by word of mouth? Can you offer discounts to existing customers if they refer a friend? How else can you encourage them to spread the word about our business/career?

In my purse, I have thirteen coffee shop loyalty cards. Thirteen! Even I was surprised when I counted them out. There are ones that I use in Dorset, Cornwall, London, Turkey, and at the airport. Not only do they tell a story about my working life, but they also tell a story about my life as a coffee customer. I'm the type of customer that likes to feel part of the community. If I have the choice between two coffee shops and one of them I have a loyalty card for, I'm going to go to that one. For me it isn't about collecting the tokens to receive a free coffee (although that's a bonus); for me, it is more about feeling loyal and part of that community. I want to give them my money because they have made me feel part of the gang. You may not feel the same way as me, and for you, it is all about collecting the tokens for that free cup of coffee. Understanding how your customers think will help you work out how to sell and keep them.

We are now going to come up with a marketing campaign to

attract new clients and customers. Start with what problem you are going to solve for them by buying your product or service. Is it that your paintings offer a lifetime of pleasure and won't fade like the prints most people have been purchasing? Do they worry that they buy artwork it doesn't look right when they get home? Can you offer a service that allows them to live with it for a week? Maybe they worry about spending all their monthly income on one piece of art. Can you offer a monthly payment plan? Or did your dance class create great results for previous clients? Did they lose weight in a fun way, or discover that they could make new friends while having fun?

Start your campaign with the problem that your clients and customers have, and then work backwards to how you are going to fix it for them. Write your results down. By starting with a problem, you get into the mindset of your customers. As customers ourselves we make all of our purchases based on a problem we have. It might be as simple as not having a new outfit for a big event, or that you need a strong cup of coffee to wake up in the morning. Or it might be something bigger, like fear of speaking in public or a need to lose weight for health reasons. Once we understand the problems of our audience, we can help them fix it.

Choose one of the problems that you believe your product or service can fix. Work out how you can describe how you will solve that problem for your client. Write it all down in as much detail as possible. Do you have any testimonials from previous clients or customers that you can use to demonstrate that you have fixed the problem before? Remember we said that testimonials build trust. To attract new clients and customers, you need to show them that you are trustworthy, that you are the right person to help them with their problem and that you have a way of proving you can do it.

Looking back at everything you have written, which bits stand out for you? Which bits do you think you could weave into a marketing campaign?

Next, we need to think about where to put that campaign. Don't be afraid to use something as simple as a poster or leaflet if you know that your potential clients and customers will see it. They might visit a particular coffee shop or gym. Where they will see it is one of the most important things. Write down all of the places you think your customer would pick up a leaflet or read a poster.

The second thing we need to think about is the digital arm of your campaign. Are your clients and customers mainly on Instagram or Facebook? As you did for the leaflet or poster campaign, you need to think about the problem you are solving and how you can express this in a social media post. Look at social media posts that attract you. Why do you open them or read them? Do they offer an incentive or a discount?

As I said before, finding clients and customers is seven times harder than keeping the ones you already have. There is no magic to finding them; you need to put the work in, think like them, help them and retain them. Think like your customers, and if that is too hard for you to do, ask the ones you already have what made them come to you in the first place and continue to use your products or services?

Create your marketing campaign and use it for the next month. Examine what worked or didn't work. Review the results and improve on what you have done.

Tip: About selling business to Business- On of the other way to find clients and customers is by cold calling potential ones. It can feel intimidating to do it the first time. Stand up when you are speaking on the telephone to allow your rib cage to breathe. Make sure you plan out the call and that you have done your research beforehand.

Explain that you know they have problem X and that you can

fix it by doing Y. It is always good to offer them a free consultation first so that you can talk them through what you are providing. Alternatively, you can send them an email with more information. It is a similar game to negotiating, but starting cold. Make sure you review your work and marketing plan every month. Figure out what works and what doesn't. It isn't always right the first time. As with our creative careers, we need to try and try again.

15

Pitching

Whether we love standing up in front of people or it brings us out in a cold sweat, we will have to do it at some point in our careers. Remember how scared I was at the beginning with stage fright? It takes practice, but you will become more comfortable at doing it. I can't guarantee that the fear will go away, but there are ways of managing it. The best way I find to deal with pitching is to research, prepare and practice as much as you can before the event. There will be moments when you find yourself having to pitch on the spot, without any notice.

We'll come back to that type of pitching, first let's look at what we can do when we have time to prepare.

Research

You might wonder what on earth you need to research before you deliver a pitch. There are a few things that you can find out before you get to the venue. Asking how many people will be attending might sound counterintuitive to calming your nerves, but understanding how large the audience will be can change how you deliver your pitch. Talking to a panel of three or an auditorium of hundreds changes the way you stand, speak or field questions. When I speak to a panel of three, I have to answer more questions, build up a rapport with each person quickly, and often I have to stand in front of them with a slide show for the whole time. I prefer talking to hundreds than a handful. For me, I find it less intimidating if I can't look at each person in the eye. You'll only find out what works for you by trying and saying yes to pitching experience.

Let's start with the smaller panel first as that is more likely to be your first experience of pitching unless you are very brave!

Asking who will be on the panel is part of your research. You have every right to question the organisers about who they are. Once you have their names and positions, do an Internet search about them. The reason I suggest this, is that it helps you to learn more about them. Do they have the same interests that you have? Would that make it easier to connect with them in a short space of time? Have they worked in the same creative field as you, or won an award for their work?

Doing this type of research shouldn't intimidate you. Knowledge is power, even if it tells you that they have had incredible life experiences and are more qualified than you. Remember not to compare your beginning to someone's middle. Having this research also makes them more human. You have already seen what they look like, what interests they have, and where they studied; this will mean that when you first meet them, they don't appear as frightening and some of the mystique has disappeared. Occasionally your research will draw a blank. It is important when you ask who is attending the panel what their name is and where they work. Those two pieces of information should be enough to find some facts about them at least.

Once you have the facts about the panel, you need to also ask the organiser about the building. How are you going to travel there? By public transport or car? Can you park or do you need a permit?

These might seem like trivial things to be thinking about before your pitch, but these could be the make or break of your day. Rushing to a location you know little about, and finding you can't park or get in, is stressful. You need to be calm and clear-headed to deliver a pitch. Do you need to show slides? Is there equipment there that you can use or do you need to hire something? Once you have dealt with these sorts of details, it will help you to focus on the pitch.

If you are pitching to hundreds, you may have to use a handheld microphone or radio microphone. If you have to use a radio microphone, this might alter what you choose to wear. I learnt this the hard way. I was speaking at an event in Brazil. It was hot and humid, and I was wearing a floaty silk dress. I hadn't done my research, and when I arrived at the venue, I was presented with a radio microphone and had nowhere to clip the receiver/battery pack on my clothing. It meant that I had to spend the whole presentation with it in my hand. It looked awkward, and I had long leads dangling from my ear to the box in my hand. It put me off my stride, and I constantly had to swap hands when I pointed at the slides on the screen behind me. It might sound like an insignificant thing, but don't underestimate the power that the unexpected problem has on your confidence and the way you deliver your message. A little research can go a long way.

If you are pitching to hundreds, it is useful to ask the organiser if any specific VIPs will be attending and whether you should be introduced to them afterwards. Knowing who the VIPs are in the room will also help you with your pitch. They may be there with a specific policy they want to push or a question they want to ask. I've had government officials sit through one of my presentations at a time when that country's artists were struggling. I was able to talk about the benefits that artists bring to deprived areas and how they can help with gentrification. Did my talk make a difference? Only time will tell, but it was a perfect opportunity to tell government officials what I felt without them being able to interrupt me! Not all pitches will be about politics or government challenges; it's useful to know if they are in the audience though as you might have a moment to plant a seed of change.

Now that we know about the research let's think about the actual presentation/pitch. In business, we talk about the elevator pitch. It is a short pitch that you should be able to deliver between the time it takes you to step into an elevator and go up one floor. The idea is that if you met someone in a lift whom you wanted to sell your idea too, you would be able to deliver it within two minutes. Two minutes might not seem a long time to you, but if I asked you to sit in silence for the next two minutes and stare at this page, I'm sure two minutes would feel like a long time.

In society, the elevator pitch is used everywhere, on radio adverts, the blurb on the back of books, on your beauty products and the food packages. The advertising industry is an expert at it, and an excellent way to learn is to listen and read the blurbs or pitches of some of your favourite products or series.

I'd like you to write down three blurbs or pitches from products or services that you use every day. Have a look at the language they use, the structure of the pitch – is there a beginning, middle, end, and summary? Do they tell you facts about the product or service? Do they encourage you to make a purchase? When you are pitching, you are selling your idea, product or service, so to begin with; it is useful to learn from the experts.

Think about your product or service now. If you were going to describe it to someone from another country what would you say? Write down what you would say in as much details as possible. Don't worry about how it sounds at the moment. Remember perfect doesn't exist. You only need to get the information down; we can worry about the layout later.

Once you have written your description, does it sound like what you do or are offering? Have you described your values? Are there some things that you can add to what you have written, that explains more about your values and the vision for your product or services? Next, I want you to think about a problem that your product or service solves and write that down.

Finally, write down the benefits of your product or service. Why would someone come to you and not a competitor? Have a look back at what you have written. Is there something that you could use as an end statement? The end statement is a short sentence that sums up what you are offering/ doing; and as it is the last thing the person hears, it is often the most important, and it is usually the thing they remember. The rest of your pitch needs to build up to that ending. I find it easier to start with the conclusion, as I can add facts that back up my end statement. You might want to start with the start. It's entirely up to you. Through practice, you'll find a way of working that suits you.

Pull out the values that are most important to you. How will you explain what they are in an elevator pitch? Can you use case studies or testimonials as a shortcut? The opening is as important as the end, as you need to grab their attention. Try to describe what your product or service is in only two sentences.

Put all of the pieces together and write the whole pitch with a beginning, middle, and end statement. A pitch Creative Women International would look something like this:

"The CWI was set up to support, train and create networks for professional women working within the creative industries. An RBS report has shown that if more women were encouraged to become entrepreneurial an additional £1.5 billion of income for the UK could be generated. The UK creative industries create more revenue than any other industry, but budgets for the arts and arts in education are being cut. By supporting organisations like Creative Women International, we can share knowledge and train creatives in business skills so that they can successfully run their own businesses. The ethos of Creative Women International is to dispel the myth of the starving artist."

In less than two minutes I have explained what Creative Women International is and why it was set up, plus some useful statistics back up what I'm saying. You don't need to explain every facet of your product or service. A broad-brush stroke is all that you need. An elevator pitch is an introduction to what you do, with room for them to ask further questions if they are interested. For a larger pitch, you would expand on the facts, values, and results that you deliver. An elevator pitch is a great thing to start with as you can use it as a mission statement on your website, publicity or biography.

Practice your elevator pitch with friends, or record yourself on your phone so that you can hear if it makes sense, or if anything is missing. With all pitching, remember the Wonder Woman pose we learnt in the confidence section. If you do meet someone in an elevator, and there is no time to do the Wonder Woman pose, remember to keep your shoulders back and speak slowly, pacing yourself. When we are nervous, we tend to speed up our speech to get the event over and done with. Speaking quickly not only makes you appear less confident, but there is a greater chance of them not understanding what you are saying, as the speed of delivery doesn't allow them to listen with ease or make space for questions and a conversation. Learning to slow our words down takes practice. Again record yourself and see if you or your friends can understand what you are saying.

Whether you are delivering your pitch to a panel of three or a room full of hundreds it is still a good idea to make some eye contact. Eye contact tells the audience that you are speaking to them directly and allows dialogue between you and them. It can take a bit of getting used to in a room full of hundreds as you have to pick out a handful of people in the front rows and talk directly to them during the pitch with the occasional glance to the back of the room. Ted Talks are brilliant resources to see how the professionals do this. Ted.com. Most Ted talks are under eighteen minutes as scientists have shown that this is the longest amount of time we can focus on one person.

Sometimes we won't be in person when we are pitching. We may have to do it online via email or an application form. With both of these methods remember to scan them for the unconfident words we talked about in the confidence and negotiation section. Before you send the email or letter, get someone you trust to look over it, as this is your chance to pitch for something of value, so you want to get it right on the first go.

Pitching doesn't need to be painful. Remember to research, prepare and practice. Slow your delivery down and remember to make eye contact. People won't be looking to see if you are nervous if they can hear you. They will be focussing on what you are saying, rather than whether you are scared or not. Those butterflies we feel are perfectly natural. Acknowledge them and let them go. By realising that they are there to tell you that you are about to do something amazing, we can thank them for protecting us and carry on.

16

Time Management

I used to think that time management was all about making a long to-do-list, and working through each task until I reached the bottom. Experience has taught me that this doesn't work. There will never be an end to your to-do-list, and the very act of trying to work through it will cause you to stress, reduce your productivity, which in turn disheartens you. You wind up feeling overwhelmed and achieve very little. I began to analyse how I used my time during the working day, and the results would surprise me.

I started with emails first thing in the morning, reading and answering them. Then I would start one of the tasks on my to-do-list; halfway through I would check back with my emails and soon over an hour had passed. I'd return to my to-do-list and pick something I thought I could complete quickly, and then I'd dip back into email or back into what I started with first. This butterfly dance went on all day. By the evening I had put most of the work away, but I was still checking emails as I brushed my teeth, and in the morning when the alarm would ring, I'd lie in bed catching up with social media and email on my phone. By looking at how I spent my time, I realised not only was it completely ineffective, but I also never switched off! I never fully engaged in my home life and allowed my work to take over rest time as well. Only by entirely switching off can we recharge our batteries, re-examine the work we have focused on and re-schedule what we need to do for the next day.

I decided to try a new way of working, starting with how many working hours I had in a day. I then divided them into the number of hours I could give my full attention to one topic or project. More hours were given to some projects than for others, like checking email. After much trial and error, five segments seemed to be the optimum number for one day's work. I imagined those five segments as cake slices. Some slices were thinner than others, and they all came together to make a perfect cake, but none of them crossed over into the other slice. Each slice was individual and could stand on its own if removed from the cake. My day began to look like this:

Slice (1) 8-9am Check and reply to email.
Slice (2) 10-13 Write one chapter of the book, 4000 words.
Slice (3) 13-14 Break for lunch and exercise (not a slice)
Slice (4) 14-16 Work on a project for CWI
Slice (5) 16-17 Take Skype coaching call
Slice (6) 17-18 Check and reply to emails

Each day would be different, and I would focus on that task for the specified time only and not check emails sporadically. Of course, life interrupts in the form of phone calls or the post arriving. The key is to return to that same task once the interruption has passed and not be tempted to check the odd email.

Both email and social media can become a time-sucking black hole. You think you can pop on to check a couple of posts or send one email, and before you know it, hours have passed. By allowing check-in-times for emails at the start and end of the day, people get used to you replying at those times. I always make it clear that I will respond, only that it might not be immediately. If it is urgent, I'd prefer that they called me. It reduces a flurry of backwards and forwards emails, with the problems solved during one phone call rather than five emails. Some companies delete any emails sent during someone's holiday time. Although this is an extreme example, I admire their courage. We have become a slave to our own time-saving devices. It is especially hard if we work alone, as it can feel like we are connecting with the outside world.

Make sure email is on your terms and find a system that works best for you. Examine your own time during the day. Look at when you use social media and for how long. Do you reply to emails as soon as they arrive? Have you got notifications set up on your devices? What would happen if you turned them off? How many hours do you work for in a day, not including distractions or flitting between tasks?

A friend of mine reduced his hours at work down to thirty. It allowed him to leave at 3 p.m. so that he could have time with his family. He took a reduction in pay but was happy to do that to reduce his working hours. He found that he still completed the same amount of work that he had when working 40 hours. The difference was that he knew he had limited time, and so structured his working days into segments, and avoided distractions like social media, until he had finished for the day. I'm sure many office workers could streamline their hours to work more effectively. I've always wondered if we offered to pay someone for a job rather than by the hour would they finish in record time and have the extra time as a vacation. As long as they completed the job, I don't think it matters if they did it quickly or not. Radical thinking, but it might enhance society's work patterns and make for a happier population.

As a working mother, I know that nothing makes you focus on your time management more than a sleeping baby. Knowing that you only have a few minutes or hours to complete a task makes you use those hours wisely. Having an endless amount of time fools us into thinking it is just that - endless. Endless is the worst thing for achieving your goals. With no end in sight, how do you know when to stop or when to review what you have done?

Think about your working week; how would you plot out those five slices of time? When are you going to check email, in the morning, afternoon or evening? Are you going to schedule your social media or upload content during the day? How many hours can you focus on one creative project or write a proposal? Understanding your attention span will help you greatly. You might be more of a morning person and work best then.

Trying to do everything only ends up with you doing several things poorly. You end up with unfinished tasks or worse still; you end the day exhausted with little or nothing to show for it.

Tip: Remember to add 30-minute gaps between meetings or appointments. Those 30 minutes allow you time to follow up what you discussed with an email while it is fresh in your head. It also allows you time to review what was said and action a couple of the points. We can forget how long we need to get to and from meetings. My philosophy is that it is always better to arrive with enough time to have a coffee, calm myself, do the wonder woman pose, and attend the appointment, rather than rushing in a flap, or worse still, late.

Don't ever arrive early to an appointment though. Those people are busy and have a specific time slot set aside for you. It can become embarrassing for both parties if you are forced to wait for them. Much better to walk around the block, listen to a podcast or grab a coffee than hover in the lobby.

You might be interested to know that time management could be the make or break of your career. Professor Angela Duckworth is a professor of psychology from the University of Pennsylvania. She has done a Ted Talk viewed by millions and written a book called 'Grit:

The power of passion and perseverance.' When we work through tasks, rather than putting them off until later, we actively engage with our grit. Grit is the determination we have to keep going even when something feels hard or impossible, rather than dropping it and telling ourselves that we will get back to it later. There will be some days when we want to bury our heads in the sand, or we get frustrated by the lack of progress we are making. Professor Angela Duckworth says that determination and single-mindedness almost always win over natural talent and moderate drive. You might know of a painter, photographer or dancer who is more talented than you but hasn't made a success of their career. It could simply be down to them not managing their time effectively or giving up when something became too hard.

Grit is what gets you through when the times are tough. It doesn't mean that you will always pick yourself up and keep going. You need to filter everything you do through the grit spectrum. If you need to take a second job to fund your art exhibition, do it with the same amount of passion as you would your art work. They both feed into each other. Can you think of a time when you have used grit and determination to get through a challenging project or experience? Think about what you did. If you gave up, what did you give up? Was there something that you could have done differently? If grit is the key to success, what can you do to cultivate it? Where can you get support to keep going when times are tough? Would an accountability partner help, or friends, family, or an online Facebook group? Knowing where to get support before we falter can help us have a greater chance of succeeding in the long run.

If we don't know how to do something, rather than despairing or feeling that we can't move forward, we can ask for help. Whether it is to learn a new piece of software, apps or merely to chat through a problem, it is essential to recognise these moments when we could use more support rather than giving up altogether. Knowing your weaknesses and what to do to support yourself, can help you to move closer to the finishing line and succeeding.

If an accountability partner would help you, there are set ways of working with one. You don't even need to work in the same industry. The basic rules of having an accountability partner are that you don't tell each other what to do. You ask open questions to try to get them to come up with a solution to the problems themselves. For example, you would ask questions like "who can help you with this problem right now"? Or "What solutions can you think of to help you? If time or money was no problem what could you do"? You are there to guide each other rather than tell each other what to do. The aim of having an accountability partner is to do at least two sessions so that you can implement what you have spoken about in the previous session. Some people find that they want to meet in person or over Skype once a week, once a month or every two months. Work out what works best for you. You don't want it to become a chore or something you dread rather than looking forward to.

Time management and how we plan for success is very personal. You need to find out what helps you the most. It is so easy for us to compare ourselves to others and panic if we aren't as productive, successful or as busy as them.

There will always be someone who is more successful or more talented than us. The key is to build grit, determination and a belief in your talents. No one else sees the world as you do. Each experience and life we live is unique to us. Your siblings or partner won't even experience the same event in the same way as you. That is a beautiful thing and something to value as it means that no one else can do exactly what you do, which means that what you are offering the world is unique. Never worry that someone else is doing the same thing. Focus on what you do differently and why people would come to you rather than them. Don't ever copy. No one wants to be remembered as a poor imitation. It is more important that people remember you for what is uniquely you.

17

Creative Breaks

There will be some point in your creative career when you hit the proverbial wall. You feel tired, all hope has gone, or you suddenly find that you no longer love what you are creating. (I usually feel like this when I am tired or have been trying to cram in too much). No matter what the cause is, the outcome is always the same – you feel like giving up. Many artists and entrepreneurs talk about this moment. It is the moment that can create success or failure. What you do next determines whether you carry on or not.

When I was a young photojournalist, I burnt out. I'd been building my career in London, shooting stories in Africa, America and Europe, while working ridiculous hours. I suddenly found myself so paralysed with fear that I couldn't take another picture. There was no rational explanation for it, apart from my own burn out which manifested itself as a sudden severe lack of confidence. My work had been published in the top magazines and newspapers like Marie Claire, and the Guardian and The Royal Photographic Society had released a double page spread about me and my work, naming me 'one to watch – coming up fast!'

I realised I needed a creative break. I also re-evaluated what I wanted from my career, and discovered it was people. I looked at the skills I had, the areas I was strongest in, and retrained as a camerawoman. I worked in documentaries for the BBC. I now work as a production manager for feature films and as the CEO of Creative Women International. I love the teams I work with and feel much happier. I still shoot photographs but on my terms. A complete career change might not be for you, but a creative break might help pull your career up to the next level.

Creative breaks can inspire new projects, build your networks and create new opportunities. As creatives, we can work 24/7 on our careers. Work comes home with us, and we think about it all the time. Creative breaks can top up our fuel tanks.

Here are some ways that you can gain positive results from creative breaks:

1. Build breaks into your calendar. They can be for one day or one week. Make sure you schedule them so that they happen.

2. During your break, be actively creative. If you spend the day walking in parks and drinking coffee, look at the people around you. Collect leaves to inspire you, listen to conversations others are having. Being actively creative allows your mind to wander and you may find a solution or new ideas to feed into your creative practice.

3. Once a year, volunteer to assist someone you admire. I call it 'working with my heroes.' They may not even work in your field. I spent a blissful week working in Rob Ryan the paper cut artist's studio. I learnt new ways of organising my own business, as well as being inspired by his creative practice. For these sorts of experiences, I save up during the year so that I can afford to do them. I treat them as a working holiday. I always return refreshed, inspired and with lots of new ideas.

4. Identify other creative ways of working. If you are a writer, maybe you enjoy painting as a past time. If you are a dancer, perhaps you enjoy writing poetry. Whatever it is, save up so that you can take a weekend class in it. The act of doing something different that you have a creative interest in can help to bring new life to your creative practice. You might be lucky enough to meet fellow creatives who form part of your support network.

Don't feel guilty! Stopping to take inspiration from another source isn't being lazy or time wasting. It is fuelling your creative tanks allowing you to carry on with your creative career.

Think about other creative interests you have, even if you have never tried them, you might find sewing exciting but have never been on a sewing machine. Or you were good at writing poetry when you were at school, but haven't written a word since. Choose something that makes you feel excited or that you want to learn. Have a look in your local area. Is there somewhere that is running classes in this activity during the next six months? Or is there an exhibition or poetry slam that you could attend as a member of the audience? Taking small steps, to begin with, allows you to try things without a huge commitment.

In Julia Cameron's book 'The Artist's Way', she recommends doing 'morning pages' to help with the creative blocks. Morning pages involve you waking up and immediately writing a stream of conscious onto blank pages. The words are part of your unconscious thinking. I've tried it a few times, and it helps with creative blocks. If that doesn't sound like something, you will enjoy, even visiting a gallery or writing down three simple positive things you think each day, can help enormously.

As creative creatures, we need to look after our inner energy levels. We are our work, and our work is us. It is a balancing act we have to perform each day to build a successful career doing what we love. Make sure you schedule time during the year to nurture that side of you. It is important to continue to be inspired and love your creative practice.

The next thing I want to talk about is Passion Projects (I touched on these earlier). Passion Projects are different from creative breaks. Passion Projects are still based around the creative work you do as part of your career. The main difference between the work you do every day and Passion Projects is that there is no client or customer for them. The whole point of Passion Projects is that they should fire the passion in your practice. You should feel excited about them or interested in something about them.

For example, most photojournalists have a Passion Project running alongside the regular work that they do for clients or commissions. It might be a story or subject that they are interested in, but a newspaper or magazine wasn't ready to commission it. Or it might be a subject the photographer cares deeply about and feels inspired to shoot a story around it. Sometimes these passion projects can take years or decades to finish. The photographer probably wasn't thinking it would take that long when they set out to take the first photograph. If they did, they would probably never have started. You might be a fashion designer who is interested in revising an old craft or developing wearable technology because you have an interest in it. Or you are an artist who is inspired to paint a small picture each morning over coffee. Whatever it is, you must care deeply about it and forget about doing it for money.

Not having an audience or client for this sort of work is very important. Once we attach an audience or client to something, it changes the way we work. We may unconsciously begin to edit or censor the way we approach the project. We might start worrying about finances rather than the subject matter. The moment money links to a creative project it changes. The passion we felt becomes a secondary consideration as the money (or worry about the client) takes over. When we come up with ideas or begin to design something we don't start with the money. If we did, then we would already be restricting our creative process.

In the beginning, we need to feel free to explore all creative avenues and ideas. We need to believe that anything is possible and then worry about finding an audience for it later. You can't do this with every project; otherwise, you would end up broke. However, the importance of Passion Projects is to find that spark you first felt as a child or young adult when you tried your creative practice for the first time. When we are spending every day chasing clients, the money, or trying to build our career, we can lose the spark. The spark is our most important asset. It's the thing that keeps us going when times are tough, or brings new inspiration to a tired project. Passion Projects have another benefit as well; they can bring you new clients and audiences.

There was a story about a young man who shot an alternative campaign for a product he admired. He felt that the person who made the advert hadn't done a great job and that they could do better. He loaded his film up online, and it caught the attention of the advertising company who had commissioned the original advert. They hired him on the spot.

I'm not saying that this is a magic pill for making all your wishes come true, but if you want something you need to show that client you are capable of delivering what they want, even before they have hired you. (This is especially true if you are starting in your creative career, and need to make a name for yourself). Some people might view this as a depressing way to do business, but if you are passionate about something you'll enjoy the process of creating something. And if that something then becomes a calling card for new clients and customers, your Passion Project has turned into so much more. The key is not to think of an end goal when you are working on a Passion Project. Otherwise, you lose the spark, and it will show in your work. We often produce our best work when we enjoy the process of pure creation. What we do with it afterwards is entirely up to us, but it should never be the reason for creating it in the first place.

If time or money were no object, what would you love to create? Write down in as much detail as possible what you would do. Does it involve bringing a team together, working with other creatives or one of your heroes? Is it a project that you have been thinking about for a while?

Look back at what you have written. What one thing could do now to make a start on this project? Is it a phone call, or creating a new contact? It doesn't have to be complicated. Write down that one thing. Is there some part of it that you can start now without worrying about money or time? Can you schedule it into the next month so that you have time to play with it, and develop a plan? Scheduling it permits you to donate time to it. If you are still worried about the money, chat with your accountant, as some of it might be tax deductible if it enhances your work or future career progression.

It is important for us to give ourselves permission to be creative even if it isn't going to earn us money. You don't want to reach burn out or lose the thing you were most passionate about. Nurture your creativity; it is the most valuable thing you own.

18

Moving On – Planning for Growth

How to network like a queen.

Once we have the foundation of our business and creative career sorted out, we can think about growing. There is a misconception that you don't need to continue growing if you have enough customers and clients. Things change. One of your clients could find themselves out of business, or the relationship you forged with a particular person at a company is lost when they move on.

Whether we enjoy it or not we need to keep making connections. The best way to do it is by networking. Networking can be a positive or painful experience depending on how you approach it.

There are different types of networking that I want you to consider to help your creative career flourish and grow. The first type is the more traditional networking experience. You attend an event with other like-minded people, and you try to make contacts with a drink in your hand. Without some preparation and an idea of what you want to get out of the event, they can either be a waste of time or a goldmine. You can start by using a platform like Eventbrite to see what networking opportunities are in your area. You can search by subject or by location. I always think it is a good idea to start local and build up from there. No matter what stage of your career you are at, it always helps to build a local support network.

Once you have decided what event you would like to attend, your homework begins. These are the points you need to consider before you attend the event.

1. What do I want to get out of attending this event? Is it new contacts, clients or support? What am I offering as an attendee, is it knowledge, sharing my connections and network?

2. Can I get to the location easily? Is there parking if I need to drive? How long will it take me to get there?

3. For support, is there another creative I would like to come with me?

4. Who else is going to be attending? How can I find this out? Contact the organiser to ask who would be a good contact for you to make at the event. Can I identify three attendees I would like to connect with?

5. Bring business cards, leaflets or examples of my work that I can carry in a small bag.

Knowing who is attending the event can help to calm your nerves. You can see if there is a particular person that would be beneficial for your career. By identifying a couple of people, you don't need to talk to the whole room. There is an idea that it is better to be fashionably late to events, which might work for parties, but in a networking situation, this can play with your nerves. It is much better to arrive on time, connect with the host and say hello to individuals as they arrive. Walking into a room full of chatting people is much harder to penetrate. Groups appear closed off, or you feel awkward trying to join in the conversation a couple of people are having. Understanding some basic body language is an excellent short cut into a group.

If a couple is squarely facing each other, with their feet pointing towards each other, this is a couple that is fully engaged with each other. There is no point trying to join them. If there is a group of people and you would like to join the conversation, look at the way the circle has formed and find a gap you can enter, then talk to one of the people on your left or right to discover what they are talking about, and join in the conversation.

Understanding the basics of body language will help you to navigate the room. If you have arrived early, ask the host to introduce you to people. It is then much easier to navigate the group of attendees. Make sure you move around the room during the event.

If all of this feels too scary take a networking buddy. I have had some brilliant nights networking with a friend. We both pick someone in the crowd that we would like to speak to, and then go and introduce ourselves. I present my friend, and my friend introduces me. It is much easier to do it this way, and much more fun. If we find we aren't enjoying the conversation with someone we have met, we move on together without feeling uncomfortable. I should note here that if you are feeling trapped in a conversation, you don't want to be part of, making an excuse to visit the bathroom works wonders. You can then return to a different group when you come back into the room.

If you do some research beforehand and are clear about what you want to get from the evening, it can become a pleasurable rather than painful experience. Think of it as a chance to make new friends and contacts. After the event, if you have collected some business cards drop them an email saying that you enjoyed meeting them and follow up with something you can connect with, like a project or something you think they would find interesting based on the conversation you had.

If someone gives me a business card before I leave the event, I scribble what we talked about, where I met him or her, and the date. This information helps me in the future when I am trying to remember where I made that contact. Knowing what you talked about helps you to write a more personal email, and tells them that you were interested in what they talked about — sending the email shortly after the event is important. It helps to build on the connection you made.

The next type of networking I want you to consider is online. It might feel strange to do your networking inside the digital world, but it can also help you to connect communities and leaders in their fields that you would struggle to access through face to face networking channels. A comfortable place to start is with Facebook groups. A quick search on Facebook will help you to find a group based on your interests. There are ones for photographers, working mums, and Creative Women International. Some groups are closed, which means you have to send a request to be added to the group. It depends on the creator of the group whether you gain access or not. It is good to start with ones that are open to anyone. Choose something that would be beneficial for your career, whether it is support or new customers/clients.

There are some rules of etiquette in these groups. No one likes to have a know-it-all at the party or someone who keeps shouting about their achievements; this is the same for these groups. You need to image them as a big party or networking event. Behave as you would at home. The best and most productive ways to gain connections in those groups is by offering to answer questions in them. Make yourself an expert before you start trying to sell them anything. If it is about making clients and customers, show your value before you pitch to them. People are more likely to purchase from someone they trust. If you can give some information away or answer questions and offer help, those groups are going to respond more positively towards you. When you have built up enough of a reputation in the group you can offer them a deal that is only available for those in the group. They will feel loyal to you, and your services as you have been building trust and showing your worth.

I have known several businesses that have gained all of their clients and customers from groups like this. It takes a while to build trust, but the rewards can be worth it. Make sure you identify groups that have your types of customers and clients in them. Don't spread yourself too thin by joining several groups at the same time. You are going to have to commit to engaging in the group regularly, so make sure it is a group you have an interest in and will enjoy the interactions regardless of whether they become new clients and customers. A word of warning here, make sure you check the rules of the group as to whether you can self promote in them, or sell your work before you upset the administrator of the group.

You might be looking for a support network rather than new clients, and these groups can offer that. The Creative Women International has a closed group as well as a public page. I have seen fantastic support and interaction happen within the group. One woman in the UK was holding an exhibition and had been let down by someone who was going to show footage of Argentina. A member from Brazil joined the conversation and said that she would contact a fellow filmmaker in Buenos Aires. Within an hour the woman in the UK was able to show footage from Argentina. It is those magic moments that can happen in these sorts of groups. People offer help for free as you are part of their community. If you choose groups that are local to you as well, there are opportunities for face-to-face meetups as well.

Always start with two questions.

1. What can I offer these groups?
2. What do I need from this group?

Make sure you are giving more than you are taking, as this will make people warm to you, and appreciate you being part of their community.

The same principles apply to LinkedIn groups. LinkedIn can help you to connect with leaders in your field. Again you are playing the long game. As before, work out what you can offer and gain from being part of the group. People are much more used to interacting in this way via digital platforms and are used to doing business and making recommendations online. You might be surprised that 100% of my film work has come from a connection or recommendation that someone made about me. The jobs were never advertised. You may think this is the wrong way to do business, but sadly it is common across all industries. People want to work with people they like, trust, or that someone has recommended. I am unusual, in that I have no family connections in the film industry. It shows that it is possible to break into difficult creative industries; you only need to have determination and networking skills. If you want something, I believe you can always find a way to achieve this.

Networking should be part of your career strategy for the rest of your career. Even if you end up in a full-time job at an organisation like the BBC, you should still network to build new contacts and to plan for the future. Company structures change, people move departments or companies. Making networks in departments other than your own is crucial. Not only does this help your career, but it also makes you a valuable employee. So often people stick to their departments. Making connections in other areas can help you to create bridges, and find out about other opportunities, or even create collaborations. Life is more interesting when you build networks in other areas. I have networks across the media industries but also in theatre, design, architecture, green issues and science, to name a few. I have enlightening conversations with all of those connections. They feed into my work in ways I couldn't have imagined if I only stuck with filmmakers.

As you move on with your career, you might find that you would like to collaborate with another creative. Collaborations can bring all sorts of benefits. They connect you to other networks, draw attention to new clients and customers or give you a big dose of creative inspiration. Collaborations can be great if you communicate with each other. Drawing up a simple agreement will make sure you understand what you both hope to get out of the collaboration. It also prevents misunderstanding and time wasters. It should foster a professional and fun partnership for the length of the project and beyond. Be clear what you both hope to gain from the collaboration and the period you want the collaboration to last. Make sure you future proof your creations as well. By that I mean who has the rights to any future income generated from the creative work. Do you have equal rights to the profits? Can you both have your name on the work in perpetuity? They might feel like uncreative things to discuss when all you want to do is create. Being clear about the financial and personal responsibilities of the collaboration will prevent problems in the long run.

The penultimate thing that I want to talk about is your online presence. It is essential to have a website, even if it is made up of one page. Sites are your shop windows. It is a way for future clients and customers to find you, or for previous customers to keep up to date with what you are offering. Without a website, it is harder to build your career. How many times have you Googled someone before you worked with them or bought from them? People will be doing the same thing when they meet or want to hire you. Having no web presence will make people question your professional history. Why don't you appear in Google searches? Why do you not have a website?

Having a web presence builds trust. It shows what you have done before. It shows that people enjoyed the experience (through testimonials.) It is a way for people to contact you.

I have had many jobs from people finding me through my website. Do not underestimate the power of an Internet search. If you are trying to attract new clients and customers, it is essential to think about this strand of your business. Think of it as marketing. You might feel that you are no good at tech, or can't put a website together, and have no money to pay someone to do it. To get you started, you only need a one-page website which you can make from free or for a few hundred pounds. Or you can hire a developer to create something for you. If you do opt for a single page, make sure it contains a biography, an example of your work, and a way to contact you. It doesn't have to be perfect. The important thing is that people find you.

About Page

Your about page is one of the most important pages on your website. It is effectively your biography. Most people write in the third person; you might prefer to write in the first person. It depends on what works best with your brand. Start with a brief two-line summary of your career so far. Pull out the best achievements you have made. If you've won an award for your work, then you can say you are an award-winning photographer, artist etc. You don't need to name the award unless it's an Oscar or Pulitzer Prize! Two lines should be all you need. Follow this up with why you do what you do. Where does your passion lie? And finally, sum up why someone would have you rather than your competitor. What is your unique selling point?

If you are starting out you can mention where you studied, or a project that you are creating. An about page should highlight you in the best light. It is a blurb about you. The same type of thing you would read on the back of a novel. Shorter is better than waffling on. You want to gain their interest rather than boring them with a lengthy CV. Have a look at your competitors' About Me pages. How have they laid it out? How long is each paragraph? Have they included a testimonial and a photograph? As you create your about page, think about where else can you use this biography? Would it work on your LinkedIn profile as well? Keep it short and sweet. Each word should be adding value if it doesn't take it away.

The Future

Finally, I want you to focus on the future. What goals do you want to achieve in the next week, month, year or three years? Look back at what you wrote at the beginning. What goals did you hope to accomplish? Now that you have begun to think about all aspects of your creative career think about your goals for the next week, month, year and three years. Only by having something to aim for can we achieve it. They might be personal goals as well, like a new car or to own your own home. To achieve those goals you might need to increase your sales and clients. Not an impossible task, but you need to plan and build a strategy to reach them.

As you move forward with your creative career, remember that what you have to offer the world is unique to you. Even if there is someone else producing something similar, it is your unique vision and talent that will make your product or service different.

We can carry on being creative beings, but without a basic understanding of how business works, we can't build a sustainable future.

Believe in your own worth. Value the time you take to complete a piece of work. Explain to clients and customers the value you are bringing to them. Be strong and stand by your values. Share your knowledge, make connections and protect your creative spark.

Art and creativity make the world go round. Without it, we would become machines. Your talent and creativity lights up the world long after you have gone. That, my friend, is something worth celebrating.

Acknowledgements

There are several people that I would like to thank in helping to make this book possible. The first is my husband Paul Irish, who has been a rock of support for me, and my biggest cheerleader. I couldn't have done this without you. The second is my son Huxley. I hope that you grow up in a world where men and women support each other to be the best that they can be. You are my sunshine.

Bill and Sheena Clarke, you have been lifelong inspirational, support and I feel blessed to have you in my life. Uncle Fred and Anke, you have been my best cheerleading team, showing me that anything is possible with hard work and dedication.

To my brother Josh, thank you for reminding me that Mum would be proud of us both. My Goddaughter Madeline, this book is for you, and I love watching you grow into such an amazing woman.

This is also in memory for my mum who showed us that creativity is everywhere and that you can build a business from home, for my Grandma Grace for being the bad-ass woman you were, and taught me so much, for Barbara and the quiet encouragement that sent me on this path, for Great Aunt Ettie and the cheeky view of life that I hope to inherit, and my Dad Ron for telling me that the 9-5 wasn't for me.

Suzy Almond, Bex Shaw, Niki McCretton, Rosie Russell, Aslan Shand, Autumn-Dawn Blanchette, Emily Dykes Tosh, and Robin Dick, you are my dream team! Thank you for being such amazing women in my life. Alice Blogg thank you for those creative coffees, they got this book finished! Dom Brown and Bearkat cafe in Bridport, and Lisa Loader and Soulshine, I wouldn't have finished without your flat-whites and toast.

To Paul Blow for your fantastic illustrations and nailing the cover.

Paul Jarvis, I wanted to thank you for inspiring me to start a podcast all those years ago. To my old team-*Percy and his angels*, who I miss working with: Percy Emmett, Nicky Margieson Schllander, Daxa Parmer, Megan Powell Vreeswijk and Alison Grade.

To Balboa Press for your support and calm manner on the telephone.

To all my amazing Creative Women International ® members, you inspire me everyday, and bring so much joy to my life.

About the Author

Philiy Page is the Founder of Creative Women International ® which was set up to support, train, and inspire creative women to create successful careers.

Philiy has worked in the creative industries for over 24 years. She started as an award winning photojournalist for publications like The Guardian and Marie Claire, before moving on to BBC documentaries, advertising, picture editing, book publishing, and working as a feature film production manager.

She has been a Teaching Fellow of entrepreneurship at the University of Bristol, and continues to deliver creative business start up courses, around the world, for Nesta & The British Council. She also delivers remote mentoring for start-ups in countries like the Ukraine, Brazil, Turkey, New Zealand and the UK.

Philiy is an invited RSA Fellow for the work she does for Creative Women International, and her mission is to dispel the myth of the starving artist.

When she's not working on Creative Women International, you can find her drinking good coffee, hiking up mountains or playing tea parties with her young son Huxley.

Photo by Paul Irish